THIS USED TO BE
PHILADELPHIA

NATALIE AND TRICIA POMPILIO

Library of Congress Control Number: 2020950051

ISBN: 9781681063126

Front cover:
Top: Philadelphia City Hall, public domain, wikipedia.org.
Bottom: Farm Journal Building, photo by Tricia Pompilio.
Back cover:
Natalie Pompilio's photo: Tricia Pompilio
Tricia Pompilio's photo: Karen Schanely Photography

Printed in the United States of America
21 22 23 24 25   5 4 3 2 1

DEDICATION

For Dad
Lou Pompilio
August 11, 1941 – May 4, 2020
Legends never die

ACKNOWLEDGMENTS

I'd like to thank my sister, Tricia, for joining me in this project and for always being by my side. T, remember: If you're going through Hell, keep going.

Special thanks to Kristen Graham, editor extraordinaire, and Lisa Wathen, semi-professional cheerleader. Rocky, you are so missed.

Much appreciation to the neighbors who shouted encouragement from their decks and the friends who did the same via Zoom. Although I haven't been able to hug them in months, I've felt the supportive embrace of the Savarese, Paxson, and Barnett/Fletcher clans. Team Paxson—Will, Maddy and Nora—I miss you. Now please stop growing. Team Savarese—Fiona, Luna, and Poppy—I can't imagine a world without Violet, Kook, Liz, Daughter, and Ratface. You always make me laugh.

Finally, an all caps THANK YOU to my husband, Jordan Barnett. He tells me I'm talented when I don't think I am and encourages me when I want to give up. I would never have been able to finish this— or get through this year or do much of anything, really—without his love, support, and understanding. Jordo: Over rainbows, through stars.

—Natalie

First, thank you goes to my sister, Natalie, who somehow managed to con me into this project. It's been a rough year, but our mutual love for Alfredo and our shared horror as we dug through boxes of paperwork (Don't forget the attic!), plus your countless calls to Opti and Comcast and ability to make me smile on the darkest of days has made it ok.

Thank you for driving me through less-than-pleasant neighborhoods and making me laugh while doing it. As Dad used to sing, "You'll Never Walk Alone."

I'm thankful for the support of friends and family near and far who never fail to show up when I need them. My gratitude cannot be expressed in words, but I appreciate all of you more than you know.

Albus and Clara, my tween cats, thank you for always making me smile.

To my husband, Vince Savarese, and our three daughters, Fiona, Luna, and Poppy, you are my strength and heart. I love you.

Lastly to Dad. I miss you terribly but know you are with Mom and with me every day. Whenever I'm overwhelmed or scared, I think of you saying, "It's no big deal. Just keep hustling, baby. Better days are coming." And suddenly I'm less afraid, empowered, and ready to take on the world.

—**Tricia**

CONTENTS

INTRODUCTION

No other American city is as perfect for a "This Used to Be" book than Philadelphia.

It's an old city by US standards, home to natives for thousands of years before European settlers arrived in the 1600s. It's the birthplace of the nation, where the documents that govern us today were crafted and where the first president lived and worked. It has played a critical role in the country's economic growth, once serving as its busiest port and later earning the nickname the "Workshop of the World" thanks to the factories that produced everything from locomotives to linens. The modern city is a hive of medical and pharmaceutical research, a growing force in the world of technology, and a center for arts and entertainment.

Most of the places and spaces featured in this book are in the greater Center City area. I chose those locations because this area is easily walkable and it's where out-of-towners are most likely to visit.

This book is a little different from others in the series because it was written during the COVID-19 pandemic of 2020, when visits to libraries and museums were forbidden. I had to rely on internet-based research and books and documents I had from writing my last book about the city, *Walking Philadelphia: 30 Tours Exploring Art, Architecture, History, and Little-Known Gems* (Wilderness Press, 2017).

The increasing digitalization of history made this easier than I'd imagined. I lost myself in the city's stories during the locked down months of spring, summer, and fall. It was a thrill to imagine W.E.B. Du Bois living and working only blocks from me, to find out a prison that housed Al Capone once stood where I buy groceries, and to learn the shot tower across from my sister's house churned out ammunition during the Civil War.

I tried to picture the non–English-speaking Italian men arriving at the Washington Avenue Immigration Station in the late 1880s with slips of paper reading "Palumbo's, 8th and Catharine." That note told authorities to point the newcomers toward the South 7th Street boardinghouse that would welcome them. During that mile-long walk, the men passed near my house.

I now walk the same streets, follow the same unseen paths. All of those who came before me had some impact on the city that exists today. I wonder what my own impact will be.

Poe Slept (Off a Bender) Here

Take away the bustling Acme supermarket and imagine a castle-like structure surrounded by 40-foot-tall stone walls. For more than 125 years, this corner housed Moyamensing Prison, a three-building complex where Edgar Allan Poe slept off an alcoholic bender, Al Capone stopped in, and America's first known serial killer, H.H. Holmes, was hanged.

The prison—alternately known as the 11th Street Dock, the Jug, and the County Hotel—was designed by Thomas Walter, who also designed the US Capitol dome. It opened in 1835; one observer wrote that it looked like it had been built "for the ages."

Most of Moyamensing's inmates were short timers. Poe spent a night in 1849. Capone bunked in for an evening before being transferred to another facility in 1929.

H.H. Holmes was held here from his arrest in 1894 until his execution by hanging in 1896. In a confession published in the *Philadelphia Inquirer*, Holmes called himself "a degenerate" and admitted to killing 27 people. Some historians believe his actual body count was in the hundreds, with most of his victims meeting their end in his Chicago "Murder Castle."

A 1959 *Philadelphia Inquirer* article tallied 15 escapes in 25 years. That same year, three inmates busted a hole in their cell's ceiling then used a bedsheet rope to rappel the prison's 40-foot wall. The men left a message on the wall: "The food isn't fit for pigs. Also, inmates are locked

The store has some *criminally* good fried chicken. You may find yourself *arrested* by the wide variety of products. You could spend a *life sentence* checking out all of the store's offerings.

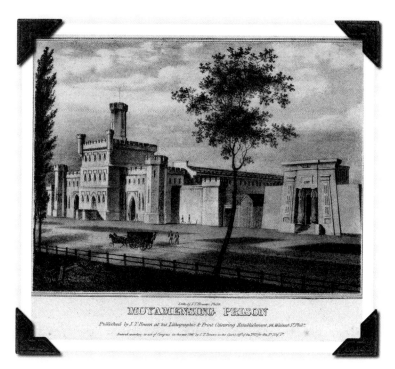

When Moyamensing Prison opened in 1835, one observer said it looked like it had been built "for the ages." It was torn down in 1967 and later replaced with a supermarket. (Illustration courtesy of the Library Company of Philadelphia.)

in their dungeons for 21 hrs. a day. We all hope you tear this joint down tomorrow. Then MAYBE we'll come back."

All were recaptured. The prison was closed in 1963 and torn down in 1967. Acme moved in a decade later.

THIS USED TO BE: Moyamensing Prison

NOW IT'S: Acme Supermarket

LOCATION: Passyunk Square

Baseball as an Equalizer

Post–Civil War America was batty for baseball. Multiple teams considered Philadelphia home, playing at fields scattered throughout the city. This land once housed one of these ballfields, known as Parade Grounds, at South 11th and Wharton Streets.

The Pythians, Philadelphia's second African American team, played here. Black civil rights activist Octavius Catto, one of the team's founders, saw the baseball diamond as another place to further the fight for equality.

The well-respected Catto had played a key role in integrating the city's streetcar system. After the passage of the 15th Amendment forbidding voter discrimination based on race, he encouraged African Americans to vote.

He also played baseball, a sport he'd excelled at while studying at the Institute for Colored Youth. Catto recruited former classmates and built a team that was the best in its league. Still, the players were seen as lesser athletes because of the color of their skin. The Pythians tried twice to join all-white leagues, failing each time.

In September 1869, the Pythians played the all-white Olympics in the first recorded interracial baseball game. The Pythians lost 44–23, but there was no denying the team's talent. The *Philadelphia Inquirer* covered every inning of this "first baseball game of the kind," noting that the Pythian players "acquitted themselves in a very creditable manner, especially their outfielders, who made several very fine fly catches."

Catto was shot and killed on Election Day 1871. He was 32 years old. In 2017, Philadelphia unveiled a statue of Catto, the city's first public work honoring an individual African American.

Visit Catto's City Hall statue, located at 1400 JFK Blvd. He appears to be in motion, moving toward the ballot box in front of him. Behind him five granite pillars contain information about his life.

Team photo of the 1906 Philadelphia Giants, a team that followed the Pythians. The Giants were the "World's Colored Champions" that year and offered to play the Chicago Cubs or the Chicago White Sox, the teams that had won the major league pennants that year. Neither team responded to the request. (Photo courtesy of the National Baseball Hall of Fame Library.) Civil rights activist Octavius V. Catto co-founded the Pythians baseball team. (Image courtesy of the LIbrary Company of Philadelphia.)

THIS USED TO BE: The Parade Grounds, a baseball field

NOW IT'S: On each of the four corners: a city-owned building which houses a police station and other municipal departments, a private home, a liquor store, and a small restaurant.

LOCATION: South 11th and Wharton Streets

A Small City unto Itself

A large boulder from the Gettysburg battlefield is one of the only reminders that this West Philadelphia park once housed Satterlee Hospital, the Union Army's largest hospital during the Civil War.

The institution, in operation between 1862 and 1865, was built in a rural area on the edge of the city. Sprawled across 12 acres, the hospital had more than 30 wards and beds for 4,500 patients either in its main building or in one of the hundreds of tents that surrounded it. Witnesses described it as a city unto itself, complete with a weekly newsletter, barber shop, library, and post office.

The hospital's patient population rose by the hundreds after the second battle of Bull Run and by the thousands after the battle of Gettysburg. The injured—both Confederate and Union soldiers—arrived by steamboat or train and were taken to Satterlee via creek raft, horse-drawn carriage, or cart.

Satterlee provided high-quality care; of the 20,000 soldiers treated there, fewer than 300 died from their battle wounds. Credit for that goes not only to its physicians but also to the more than 100 Sisters of Charity who provided nursing care.

One patient later wrote that the sisters "are different from anyone else, or from other people, for they never get sick and they do for us what no other person would do. They are not afraid of the fever, small pox [sic], or anything else."

The memorial boulder from Devil's Den in Gettysburg was placed in 1915. It is in the park, partially covered by vegetation on the south side of Baltimore Avenue between 43rd and 44th Streets. A state historic marker erected in 2003 is curbside.

More than 20,000 soldiers from both sides of the conflict were treated at Satterlee Hospital during the Civil War. The facility had a remarkably high standard of care. Fewer than 300 patients died from their war injuries. (Illustration courtesy of the Library Company of Philadelphia.)

Clark Park was established in 1895. It sprawls over 9.1 acres. (Photo by Tricia Pompilio.)

Satterlee Hospital was the Union Army's largest hospital, sprawling over 12 acres in what is now West Philadelphia. The land is now a popular park. (Image courtesy of Friends of Clark Park.)

THIS USED TO BE: Satterlee Hospital

NOW IT'S: Clark Park

LOCATION: West Philadelphia

America's First Fast Food Restaurant

In 1902, Joseph Horn and Frank Hardart opened the country's first Automat in downtown Philadelphia. These coin-operated cafeterias, a German invention, showcased hundreds of fresh food items—both hot and cold—behind glass windows. Diners would choose their meals by inserting a nickel or two into the designated slot to open the windows. Workers behind the scenes would then quickly refill the spaces.

Americans immediately embraced the Automat; on its first day, the Philadelphia restaurant took in 8,693 nickels. That's $434.65, the rough equivalent of $13,154 today. Horn and Hardart expanded along the east coast, opening dozens of restaurants with heavy concentrations around Philadelphia and New York City. In 1922, one company ad claimed one out of every 16 Philadelphians ate at an Automat each day.

Another ad from the 1920s promoted the company's prepared meals which could be purchased at grocery stores with the promotional line, "Less Work for Mother."

Automats welcomed diners of all social classes, skin colors, and genders. The financially secure and those on tighter budgets dined side-by-side in the pristine, chrome-heavy, Art Deco–style restaurants. Among the customer favorites: meatloaf, macaroni and cheese, mashed potatoes, baked beans, and creamed spinach.

The Automat is now a part of the American lexicon. In the 1967 book *Rosemary's Baby*, one character says he loves Horn & Hardart's pumpkin pie. In the 1976 movie *Rocky*, the boxer reacts to being invited

Long before it housed the Automat, a print shop that served the needs of President George Washington and the new US Congress operated at this site. Long before the Automat, this site housed a print shop that served the needs of President George Washington and the new US Congress.

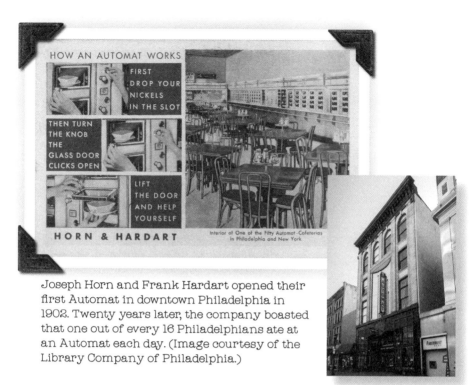

HOW AN AUTOMAT WORKS

FIRST DROP YOUR NICKELS IN THE SLOT

THEN TURN THE KNOB THE GLASS DOOR CLICKS OPEN

LIFT THE DOOR AND HELP YOURSELF

HORN & HARDART

Interior of One of the Fifty Automat-Cafeterias in Philadelphia and New York

Joseph Horn and Frank Hardart opened their first Automat in downtown Philadelphia in 1902. Twenty years later, the company boasted that one out of every 16 Philadelphians ate at an Automat each day. (Image courtesy of the Library Company of Philadelphia.)

The exterior of the first Automat is little changed, providing glimpses of its Art Deco origins. The restaurants were known for their gleaming chrome interiors where diners of all social classes, skin colors, and genders were welcome. (Image courtesy of the Library Company of Philadelphia.)

to Thanksgiving dinner with Adrian's family by saying, "Last time I had a turkey, it was when they had a special at Horn & Hardart's about three years ago." In the 2020 documentary *The Automat*, famous customers, including Ruth Bader Ginsburg, Mel Brooks, Elliott Gould, and Carl Reiner, share memories of the restaurant.

The rise of chains like McDonald's and Burger King in the 1970s and '80s led to the decline of the Automat. The last one closed in 1991.

THIS USED TO BE: The country's first Automat

NOW IT'S: Medical offices

LOCATION: Center City

Government Guided by the Will of the People

In the late 1600s, William Penn, Proprietor of Pennsylvania, lived here in the "Slate Roof House." It's where he finished his Charter of Privileges, promising settlers religious liberty and a government that was guided by the will of the people.

More than 70 years later, John Hancock, John Adams, and other members of the Continental Congress stayed in Penn's former home while expanding on his ideas to craft the first US Constitution.

The house was torn down in 1867. In 1982, Friends of Independence National Historical Park created this open-air monument to Penn to celebrate the 300th anniversary of the Commonwealth's founding. It takes its name, Welcome Park, from the seventeenth-century ship that carried Penn from England.

On the park's grounds is the city's original street grid. Penn imagined Philadelphia as a "greene country towne," with wide avenues and multiple green spaces. There's also a statue of Penn, a smaller version of the one that tops City Hall at 1400 JFK Boulevard.

Walls around the park are inscribed with Penn's words, including "By Liberty of Conscience, we understand not only a mere Liberty of the Mind, but the exercise of ourselves in a visible way of worship." and "Any government is free to the people under it where the laws rule, and the people are a party to those laws."

The Penn statue atop City Hall is actually 37 feet tall and weighs 57,000 pounds. In one hand, Penn is holding the Pennsylvania Charter of Privileges.

Philadelphia founder William Penn lived in the Slate Roof House after arriving from England in the 1600s. It's where he wrote his Charter of Privileges promising religious freedom and fair government. (Photo courtesy of the Free Library of Philadelphia's Digital Collections.)

When Penn oversaw the creation of the Commonwealth of Pennsylvania, he imagined a place where religious minorities persecuted elsewhere could worship freely. As a Quaker, he'd suffered such discrimination firsthand. (Illustration courtesy of the Free Library of Philadelphia Digital Collections.)

THIS USED TO BE: Slate Roof House

NOW IT'S: Welcome Park

LOCATION: Old City

What a Nickel Would Buy You

The Crystal Palace, a nickelodeon, opened here in 1908. Since then, the original building has had at least six major renovations and nine different names.

A nickelodeon was an indoor movie theater that showed multiple 10- to 15-minute films and charged five cents per ticket. (The name melds the admission cost and the Greek word for theater.) There were about 8,000 nickelodeons in the United States at the peak of their popularity in the early 1900s. The Crystal Palace had space for 500 people.

The creation of the full-length feature film killed nickelodeons as theater owners charged more for tickets. In the 1930s, RKO Pictures—one of the "Big 5" studios during Hollywood's Golden Age—took over the Crystal Palace and renamed it the New Palace. *Citizen Kane* was one of the RKO releases shown here.

In the 1960s, the venue was reborn as the Theatre of Living Arts, a regional repertory stage company which fostered the early acting careers of Danny DeVito and Morgan Freeman. In the 1970s, TLA was revitalized as a one-screen cinema specializing in non-mainstream films; filmmaker John Waters said the theater was instrumental in his success. TLA was the first Philadelphia movie house to offer a midnight showing of *The Rocky Horror Picture Show*.

Concert promoter Live Nation purchased the theater in the 1980s and rehabbed it to create a 1,000-capacity concert venue.

Live Nation had to remove 75 pounds of rice left from years of *Rocky Horror* showings before it could begin remodeling the interior.

The Crystal Palace Nickelodeon opened in this building in 1908. In the years since, it has also served as a movie theater, a live stage venue, and a music hall. (Photo by Tricia Pompilio.)

THIS USED TO BE: Crystal Palace Nickelodeon

NOW IT'S: Theatre of Living Arts (TLA)

LOCATION: Queen Village

The Grande Dame of Broad Street

The Bellevue-Stratford Hotel was one of the country's grandest and most luxurious hotels in the first half of the 20th century, earning it the nickname "the Grande Dame of Broad Street." The 19-story building built in the French Renaissance style had more than 1,000 guest rooms, each equipped with the technological marvel we know as the telephone. Its hallways were designed to be wide enough to accommodate women who wore six-foot-wide hoop skirts as they moved between its three ballrooms. The same space consideration was given for guests who wanted to enjoy the rooftop rose garden.

Guests included members of the Astor and Vanderbilt families; film stars, including Bob Hope and Katharine Hepburn; and almost every American president to have served since the hotel's 1904 opening during Theodore Roosevelt's administration.

The hotel hosted the Republican National Conventions in 1936 and 1948. Democrats, too, celebrated their presidential nominee here in 1948.

The hotel's luck changed in 1976 after the American Legion hosted a three-day convention. Within days, more than 200 people became ill and 34 others died from what became known as Legionnaires' disease. Experts said that bacteria breeding in the hotel's cooling tower had spread throughout the building via the air-conditioning system.

The Bellevue's website somehow manages to gloss over this aspect of the building's history, summing it up in this way: "After decades of playing a premier role in the country's hospitality landscape, the property was put up for sale in 1976 and was eventually purchased in 1978 . . . "

Visit XIX (Nineteen), the building's top floor restaurant, to enjoy fabulous city views or try happy hour at XIX's lounge. Both hint at the opulence the hotel was once known for.

The luxurious Bellevue-Stratford Hotel was called "the Grande Dame of Broad Street." Among its high-end amenities: a telephone in each of its 1,000 guest rooms. (Detroit Publishing Co. The Bellevue-Stratford Hotel, Philadelphia [Between 1900 and 1915]. Photograph retrieved from the Library of Congress, www.loc.gov/item/2016815038/.)

THIS USED TO BE: Bellevue-Stratford Hotel

NOW IT'S: The Bellevue, a multiuse property with a hotel, retail, and restaurants

LOCATION: Center City

The Building That Lasted Less Than a Week

When the Pennsylvania Anti-Slavery Society dedicated its new headquarters on May 14, 1838, former President John Quincy Adams called the new structure a place "wherein liberty and equality of civil rights can be freely discussed, and the evils of slavery fearlessly portrayed ... "

The building, called Pennsylvania Hall, was destroyed by arson less than a week later.

In the days between the building's birth and death, it hosted the annual Anti-Slavery Convention of American Women. More than 200 men and women attended. "I have found on earth a place where order, harmony, love and freedom prevail," one conventioneer wrote as she settled into the city.

That "order, harmony, love and freedom" didn't last long. Protesters surrounded the building while the delegates were meeting, jeering and throwing rocks at its windows. Conventioneers leaving at the end of the day were "assailed with stones, mud, potatoes, onions, and whatever first came to hand."

After the second day's programming, white men and women linked arms with their African American counterparts to protect them from "a mob of two or three thousand fierce, vile looking men, and large boys." This show of solidarity only further enraged the protesters. On May 17,

Quaker abolitionist Lucretia Mott organized the Philadelphia Female Anti-Slavery Society in 1833. Its nearby headquarters has now been replaced by the US Mint, at the corner of 5th and Arch Streets.

The headquarters of the Pennsylvania Anti-Slavery Society was destroyed by protesters a week after its unveiling. (Image by Bowen, J.T. & Wild, J.C. (1838). "Destruction by fire of Pennsylvania Hall, the new building of the Abolition Society, on the night of 17th May." Photograph retrieved from the Library of Congress, www.loc.gov/item/2014645336/)

a crowd of about 10,000 surrounded the empty building before charging inside and breaking anything they could grab before setting it ablaze.

Four days after its grand opening, Pennsylvania Hall was a pile of smoking rubble. It was never rebuilt.

THIS USED TO BE: Pennsylvania Hall

NOW IT'S: American College of Physicians

LOCATION: Independence Mall Historic District

"Wonderful, Marvelous, Almost Inconceivable, Yet So True"

When African American banker E.C. Brown wasn't allowed to enter a city theater because of his skin color, he decided to do something about it. In 1919, he and his business partner unveiled the Dunbar Theatre, the city's first Black-built, Black-owned showplace for African American entertainers.

Soon after its opening, the *Philadelphia Tribune* described the venue as "the finest theater in the world, owned, managed and controlled by colored people." It also became a point of pride for the city's growing African American population "that they will be and are proud of and can boast about . . . wonderful, marvelous, almost inconceivable, yet so true," the newspaper also noted.

Renamed the Lincoln Theatre in 1921 after a change in ownership, this brick building with its grand marquee offered plays, musicals, and concerts. The Lafayette Players, a company of African American actors that originated in Harlem, brought *The Shoplifters* and *The Hunchback of Notre Dame* to local audiences. Some of the biggest musical stars of the era—including Duke Ellington, Lena Horne, Cab Calloway, and Fats Waller—also performed here.

The theater was also a public meeting place. In 1938, the *Philadelphia Inquirer* reported that citizens concerned with the growing power of the

The *Philadelphia Tribune* has been in print since 1884, making it the oldest continuously published African American newspaper in the United States. Its headquarters at 520 South 16th Street is a few blocks from here.

When it opened in 1919, the Dunbar Theatre was the city's first Black-built, Black-owned live entertainment venue. It was renamed the Lincoln Theatre a few years later. (Photo courtesy of City of Philadelphia photo archive, phillyhistory.org.)

The theater was more than a show place. It also hosted community gatherings. (Photo courtesy of Special Collections at Temple University Libraries.)

Nazi Party in Germany began a meeting with the burning of an effigy of Adolf Hitler.

In 1945, the building was reborn as a Yiddish theater. The city took control of the property in the 1950s and razed the building.

THIS USED TO BE: Dunbar/Lincoln Theater

NOW IT'S: Philadelphia Board of Health facility

LOCATION: Southwest Center City

The Kid Glove Kids

Leather makers claimed this land as their own beginning in the early 1800s, sinking their wooden vats into the soft mud along the banks of the Cohocksink Creek and then using the rushing waters to wash away waste.

In 1855, Burk Brothers Tannery and Leather Factory began acquiring property here, eventually operating 12 redbrick, interconnected factory buildings on two acres. Thousands of workers processed millions of imported goat and kid skins to create soft, supple gloves. The company developed a technique that transformed the leather-making process, reducing a process that once took months to days. Burk Brothers grew to be the second largest kid glove manufacturer in the world.

The factories ended leather production in the 1960s. A vinyl record company briefly set up shop only to learn the earth beneath the buildings had become toxic. In the 1980s, the Environmental Protection Agency launched a massive cleanup. By the 1990s, a developer was planning to build condos here.

Then the developer backed out, gifting the land to the Northern Liberties Neighbors Association. At the time, it was the only city neighborhood without a significant amount of green space.

It took two weeks to take down the Burk buildings and a few years for the neighborhood group and its supporters to create Liberty Lands, a multiuse park with a butterfly garden, hundreds of trees, and several picnic and recreation areas.

The mural near the park's entrance is called *Cohocksink: Stand in the Place Where You Live*. To be fair, it was difficult to live near the creek back in the day because the land around it was unstable.

Liberty Lands Park includes a butterfly garden, a picnic area, and hundreds of trees. (Photo by Tricia Pompilio.)

Burk Brothers—Glazed Kid

Burk Brothers Tannery and Leather Factory grew to include 12 buildings sprawled over 2 acres. (Photo via Workshopoftheworld.com.)

THIS USED TO BE: Burk Brothers Tannery and Leather Factory

NOW IT'S: Liberty Lands Park

LOCATION: Northern Liberties

A Locomotive Giant in the Heart of the City

In 1832, after years of effort, Baldwin Locomotive Works unveiled "Old Ironsides," one of the first successful train models made in the United States. Crafting the steam-powered wood and iron prototype with a top speed of 30 m.p.h. was so involved that company founder Matthias Baldwin allegedly looked at the finished product and declared, "This is the last locomotive that we'll ever build."

How wrong he was. By the 1880s, Baldwin employed more than 3,000 workers and was producing about 600 locomotives a year, making it the nation's largest locomotive manufacturer. It shipped its products overseas as far as Australia and Siberia. During the Golden Age of Railroads—after the Civil War and before the start of the 20th century—Baldwin was part of the "Big Three" in steam locomotive production. Almost every rail line in the country used its machines.

Thousands of immigrants worked at Baldwin's 200-acre industrial complex in what is now downtown Philadelphia. At its busiest, the company had 17,000 laborers working around the clock.

BLW added rifle and ammunition manufacturing to its repertoire during World War I. Still, the company struggled to diversify. The growing availability of automobiles and the construction of interstate highways adversely affected its bottom line. After World War II, the increasing use of air travel and the rise of diesel and electric engines were further blows to the company's profits.

BLW built more than 70,000 locomotives until it suspended operations in the 1950s.

The founder of Baldwin Locomotive Works said Old Ironsides would be the only locomotive the company built. Instead, Baldwin became part of the "Big Three" in steam locomotive production, at one point employing 17,000 workers around the clock. (Photo courtesy of The Franklin Institute.)

Baldwin's company eventually sprawled across 200 acres of downtown Philadelphia, but that was still not big enough for the growing company, which began moving operations into the suburbs in the late 1920s. (Postcard photo of the Baldwin Locomotive Works, not mailed, circa 1900-1906. Public Domain via commons.wikimedia.org.)

Baldwin produced the last of its 70,000+ locomotives in the 1950s and shut down in the 1970s. (Image by Keystone View Company, (ca. 1905) Stripping and boxing foreign engine for shipment, Baldwin Locomotive Works, Philadelphia, Pa. Retrieved from the Library of Congress, www.loc.gov/item/91784447/.)

Matthias Baldwin was also an abolitionist who integrated his workforce and supported the education of African American children. He is honored with a statue outside City Hall, 1400 JFK Boulevard.

THIS USED TO BE: Baldwin Locomotive Works

NOW IT'S: Bustling intersection of N. Broad and Spring Garden Streets with residences, businesses, and a high school

LOCATION: Lower North Philadelphia

Keep the Cold Ones Comin'

Philadelphia was—and still is—a beer town. Schmidt & Sons was its largest and best-known brewery. At its peak in the late 1970s, Schmidt's was churning out four million barrels of beer each year. Its 1987 closure left Philadelphia without a brewery for the first time in 130 years.

Founder Christian Schmidt had apprenticed with a beer brewer in his native Germany before arriving in the United States in the 1850s. He worked as a master brewer at another Philadelphia brewery before launching his own in 1860. Two of his earliest offerings were Pilsner and Puritan.

The industry grew quickly: in 1893, the city had 26 breweries, each producing more than 15,000 barrels of beer per year. "The importance of brewing interest in Philadelphia is recognized by all. The profit shows itself in improvements, magnificent blocks and bank deposits. The city can be justly proud of its beer," the *Philadelphia Inquirer* wrote at the time.

One of the company's most memorable commercials featured the jingle: "Schmidt's is a dry beer, a mellow beer, a hearty beer, blended into one beer ... Schmidt's, one beautiful beer."

In the 1980s, Schmidt's was producing more than four million barrels of beer per year under 30 different brand names. Still, the brewery was unable to keep up with the competition. It closed in 1987.

Philadelphia's beer scene is once again flourishing. Local breweries include Yards, Dock Street, Crime & Punishment, Evil Genius, Love City, and Urban Village.

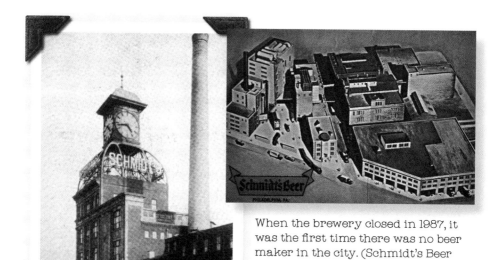

When the brewery closed in 1987, it was the first time there was no beer maker in the city. (Schmidt's Beer postcard. Public domain, via flickr.)

Founded in 1869, the Christian Schmidt Brewing Company aka Schmidt & Sons, remains the largest brewery to ever operate in the city. (The Western Brewer, May 1914. Public domain via wikipedia.com.)

A sign reading "Home of Schmidt's Beer and Ale" is one of the only clues of what this mixed-use property used to be. (Photo by Tricia Pompilio.)

THIS USED TO BE: Schmidt & Sons Brewery

NOW IT'S: The Piazza, multiuse property with residences, retail, and restaurants

LOCATION: Northern Liberties

A Profound and Powerful Painter

Painter Thomas Eakins, who died in 1916, is considered one of the most influential artists in modern American history. The Philadelphia native took realism to a new level; he was, as his biographer noted, the "first major painter to accept completely the realities of contemporary urban America, and from them to create powerful, profound art."

Eakins's best-known work is *The Gross Clinic* (1875). The detailed eight by six-and-a-half-foot work depicts well-known physician-educator Samuel Gross as he operates on a patient, a bloody scalpel in hand. A group of students stand around him. In the surrounding gallery, a distressed woman covers her eyes.

Artist Thomas Eakins was born in Philadelphia in 1844 and died here in 1916. (Detail of a 1902 self-portrait. Courtesy of the National Academy of Design, New York.)

One critic called the painting "one of the most powerful, horrible, yet fascinating pictures that has been painted anywhere in this century ... but the more one praises it, the more one must condemn its admission to a gallery where men and women of weak nerves must be compelled to look at it, for not to look at it is impossible."

Eakins was also a respected instructor at Philadelphia Academy, one of the country's best art schools. His drive for realism contributed to his resignation: During one class, he removed a male model's loincloth to trace a muscle. Victorian Philadelphians insisted he quit.

Mural Arts Philadelphia offers reasonably priced guided tours of some of its works. Visit muralarts.org for more information.

Thomas Eakins's *The Gross Clinic* (1875) shocked viewers because of its graphic depiction of an operation. The artist painted himself among the onlookers. (Courtesy of Philadelphia Museum of Art.)

With the exception of the shutters and the landscape, exterior of Thomas Eakins's house is little changed. (Photo by Tricia Pompilio.)

THIS USED TO BE: Home of Thomas Eakins

NOW IT'S: Mural Arts Philadelphia Headquarters

LOCATION: Fairmount

Jack Frost Is All In

Philadelphia was a pretty sweet city at the dawn of the twentieth century, with some of the largest sugar refineries in the world operating along the Delaware River, and more than 100 local chocolate and candy factories shipping products to thousands of stores throughout the country.

One of the first and largest refineries was the Pennsylvania Sugar Refining Company, known to locals as the "Sugar House." That was also the name of the casino that opened here in 2010 with "sugar-stick art" hanging from its ceilings, a restaurant called The Refinery, and a casual eatery called Jack's.

In the late 1800s, more than 90 percent of the country's sugar was produced in Philadelphia factories. Over the next century and under various owners, the original Penn Sugar complex grew to include 18 buildings and became a city landmark known for its 150-foot-tall chimney.

National Sugar, better known as Jack Frost, was the last company to operate the refinery, sending its product out into the world via Jack Frost-branded rail cars. In 1960, it was the world's largest sugar refinery with 1,200 employees working to process five million pounds of sugar each day.

The company went bankrupt in 1981. Hundreds of onlookers, including former employees and their families, watched as 700 pounds of explosives brought down the last of its buildings in November 1997. Construction workers clearing the site uncovered a large collection of Native American relics dating back 3,000 years. A local historian said other past uses of this land included a British Revolutionary War Fort, a shipyard, a gentleman's club, and a whale oil factory.

The SugarHouse Casino was renamed Rivers Casino in 2019 when new ownership took over the business.

Jack's Bar and Grill is still open on the property. Its menu includes several sugary delights including Key Lime Pie, Cheesecake, and Root Beer Floats.

Pennsylvania Sugar Refinery Company was the country's last independent sugar producer until it was sold to National Sugar in the 1940s. (National Sugar Refinery Company 1950s (Jack Frost Brand). Public domain via oldstocks.com.)

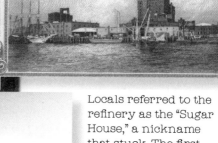

Locals referred to the refinery as the "Sugar House," a nickname that stuck. The first casino on this site bore that name. (Image courtesy of the Historical Society of Pennsylvania Photograph Collection.)

SugarHouse Casino was renamed Rivers Casino in 2019 when new ownership took over the business. (Photo by Tricia Pompilio.)

THIS USED TO BE: Jack Frost Sugar Refinery

NOW IT'S: Rivers Casino

LOCATION: Fishtown

White Teeth Courtesy of Dr. White

For 50 years, this building was the headquarters of the S.S. White Company, a dental industry innovator that still exists today. Samuel Stockton White founded the company in 1844 with three employees who hand-carved artificial teeth in his home's attic. By 1868, when the company moved into this custom-built five-story building, it had more than 300 employees, owned multiple patents, and was widely respected in the United States and Europe. It would eventually become the largest dental manufacturing company in the world.

White and his company are credited with the development of many of the first modern dental products and instruments, including the electric drill, multiple drill bits made from steel or stone that allowed for more precision, ivory-handled hand instruments, porcelain teeth that could be mass produced, and the first all-metal dentist chair. The company published a periodical called *The Dental Cosmos* from 1859 to 1939.

White was a savvy businessman, working to standardize dental education while also encouraging the use of S.S. White products. When White learned that Union soldiers needed to have at least six upper and six lower teeth to bite off the end of a powder cartridge, he met with President Abraham Lincoln to offer dental services. (Nothing came of that offer.) During World War I, a print advertisement for White's toothpaste published in the *Saturday Evening Post* boasted that "American Teeth Impress Our British Allies."

White remains one of the most revered names in his field, credited with "transforming dentistry from a secretive trade into a respectable medical discipline," according to the company's website.

The building is located in the heart of Philadelphia's "Gayborhood," which explains its rainbow crosswalks and street signs.

S.S. White exhibit. Main building. (Silver albumen print, courtesy of City of Philadelphia photo archives, phillyhistory.org.)

Dr. Samuel Stockton White was a visionary who inspired creativity in his employees. He's also credited with inspiring others in his profession. (S.S. White Dental Manufacturing Co. ad, ca 1940. Public domain, pinterest.com.)

THIS USED TO BE: S.S. White Dental Company

NOW IT'S: The White Building - Condominiums

LOCATION: Center City

A Beacon in the Sky

The 36-story Philadelphia Savings Fund Society is considered the country's first modern skyscraper. Completed in 1933 at an estimated cost of $8 million, the structure's amenities included radio reception devices installed by RCA Victor Company.

The building was the world's second tallest building to have central air-conditioning, an innovation many people feared, calling it "weather in a box." To allay concerns that central air was harmful to one's health, an engineer spent 24 hours in the building, emerging intact.

The glowing PSFS sign atop the building, visible for 20 miles, was considered odd at the time. During the Depression, some said the letters stood for "Philadelphians Slowly Face Starvation." Still, the company kept the lights on, hoping to reassure customers that their money was safe as other banks failed.

The 33rd floor was reserved for company executives. According to legend, the elevator operators would accompany the executives and their guests to the 32nd floor, then step out so the passengers could continue alone, shouting, "You're on your way, gentlemen!" as the doors closed.

Centuries before the skyscraper was built, this land housed British equestrian John Bill Ricketts's riding ring. In 1793, Ricketts presented the country's first circus, which featured jugglers and tight rope walkers along with Ricketts himself performing riding tricks, including riding two horses by standing with a foot on each. President George Washington attended one of its earliest performances.

Loews opened its hotel here in April 2000. The PSFS sign still shines nightly.

Loews's restaurant, Bank and Bourbon, features cocktails made with spirits house-aged in charred oak barrels, including Benjamin Franklin's Milk Punch cocktail, inspired by a recipe Franklin sent to a friend in the 1700s. Ingredients include milk, green tea, whiskey, and lemon juice.

During the Great Depression, some said the building's marquee stood for "Philadelphians Slowly Face Starvation," not "Philadelphia Savings Fund Society." (Courtesy of the Free Library of Philadelphia Print and Picture Collection.)

The famous PSFS building: home of the Philadelphia Savings Fund Society — one of the most modern buildings in America.

The PSFS building is one of the first modern skyscrapers in the United States. It is listed on the National Register of Historic Places. (Courtesy of Free Library of Philadelphia Print and Picture Collection.)

THIS USED TO BE: Philadelphia Savings Fund Society

NOW IT'S: Loews Hotel

LOCATION: Center City

"When His Mortal Course Was Run"

Palumbo Recreation Center's buildings and fields formerly housed the sprawling Ronaldson Cemetery.

James Ronaldson, a Scottish immigrant who made money in manufacturing, donated this land to be used as burial grounds in 1827. The remains of more than 10,000 people once rested here, including a soldier who crossed the Delaware River with George Washington during the American Revolution and Commodore Charles Stewart, Commander of "Old Ironsides" during the War of 1812.

Ronaldson designed the cemetery with two small shacks: One was to house the gravedigger. The other held the bodies of "persons dying suddenly ... the string of a bell put into their hand, so that if there should be any motion of returning to life, the alarm bell might be rung, the keeper alarmed and medical help procured," according to the book *The Lives of Eminent Philadelphians, Now Deceased* by Henry Simpson.

"Every nationality of the Old World is represented on the tombstones and monuments," an 1879 *Philadelphia Inquirer* article noted, referring to Europe. Robinson also welcomed those from the Far East, donating a plot to a Chinese immigrant, John Shou, "in which to lay his exhausted body when his mortal course was run." Shou's course ended in 1831.

The city reclaimed this space in the 1950s, replacing the bodies with ballfields.

While the center's facilities are for resident use, the adjacent playground is open to the public. It's geared toward younger children.

Ronaldson Cemetery had two buildings in its center: One for the gravedigger and the other for the newly deceased. (Image courtesy of Temple University Libraries, Urban Archives.)

Most of the land that once housed Philadelphia's dead is now ball fields. (Photo by Tricia Pompilio.)

The exterior gateway to Ronaldson Cemetery, land now occupied by Palumbo Recreation Center. (Image courtesy of Temple University Libraries, Urban Archives.)

THIS USED TO BE: Ronaldson Cemetery

NOW IT'S: Palumbo Recreation Center

LOCATION: Bella Vista

A Legacy of Caring
Inspired by Its Namesake

It's unlikely that residents of the Gratz Apartments know the complex's rich history. In the 1920s, a group of Jewish women opened a boardinghouse for single Jewish women working in the city. They called it the "Rebecca Gratz Club" to honor a local nineteenth-century philanthropist. The name is still visible above an outdoor gate.

In the decades that followed, the property served as a nonreligious halfway house for women who had been hospitalized with emotional troubles, a shelter for runaways, a place where unmarried pregnant women shunned by their families could live, and a treatment center for severely disturbed adolescent girls. A 1972 *Philadelphia Inquirer* article about the organization included an interview with a Gratz Club resident who said, "For the first time, I feel I'm worth something. I'm somebody. For the first time I think I know 'me' and where I'm going."

Gratz, who died in 1869, was a civic leader who founded the Hebrew Women's Benevolent Society in 1818 and the country's first Jewish Sunday School. Gratz was reportedly as beautiful as she was generous, turning down numerous proposals from men outside her faith. Sir Walter Scott used her as the inspiration for the female protagonist in *Ivanhoe*. Like the woman on whom her character was based, the fictional Rebecca was a beautiful, strong, and caring Jewish woman who refused to renounce her faith even when threatened with death.

Gratz was one of 12 children and many of her siblings, too, left lasting marks on the city, cofounding the nonsectarian Female Association for the Relief of Women and Children in Reduced Circumstances and establishing the Philadelphia Orphan Society.

Philanthropist Rebecca Gratz inspired generations of do-gooders, including the Jewish women who founded the Rebecca Gratz Club and named it in her honor. (Image from the Rosenbach of the Free Library of Philadelphia.)

The exterior of the Rebecca Gratz Club's building is little changed. It now houses an upscale apartment building called The Gratz. (Photo by Tricia Pompilio.)

THIS USED TO BE: Rebecca Gratz Club

NOW IT'S: The Gratz Apartments

LOCATION: Society Hill

Banquets, Bar Mitzvahs, and Baptisms

Louie Prima, Jimmy Durante, Louis Armstrong, and Bob Hope were a few of the stars who performed at Frank Palumbo's Cabaret Restaurant, which stood here for more than a century before it was destroyed by fire in 1994.

Frank's grandfather opened the building as a boarding house for Italian construction workers in 1884. Many of these immigrants arrived in the United States knowing no English but with a slip of paper pinned to their shirts that read, "Palumbo's, 8th and Catharine."

Frank Palumbo later turned the boarding house into an entertainment complex, buying adjacent properties to use as banquet halls and bars. In the 1940s and 50s, Palumbo's facilities occupied a full city block. Besides offering first class entertainment, the club was a gathering space for local families and civic organizations, hosting countless baptisms, bar mitzvah celebrations, and the annual banquet for the all-Black Old Philadelphia Club. A 1949 article in *Life* magazine focused on a single day in June when Palumbo's hosted 31 weddings.

Palumbo, as one *Philadelphia Inquirer* article noted, held "sway nightly among his innumerable friends." Frank Sinatra was one of these friends and the restaurateur was best man when the crooner married Ava Gardner in 1951 in Philadelphia. Palumbo also convinced his famous pal to sponsor a youth football team in the local midget league, which later became the Pop Warner program. In 1948, Palumbo's Clickets beat Sinatra's New York Cyclones in the first "Santa Claus Bowl," an event promoting the growing league.

Actor/singer Mario Lanza, who was born and raised a few blocks from here, once called Palumbo one of the city's "unsung heroes." The Lanza home, at 636 Christian Street, was torn down in 2018 and replaced with an apartment building.

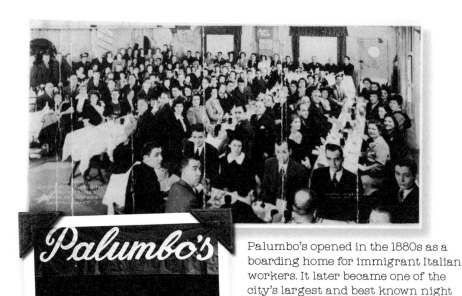

Palumbo's opened in the 1880s as a boarding home for immigrant Italian workers. It later became one of the city's largest and best known night clubs. (Public domain via facebook. com/oldimagesofphiladelphia/.)

Palumbo's Cabaret attracted stars including Frank Sinatra and Louis Armstrong. (Public domain via facebook.com/ oldimagesofphiladelphia/.)

Palumbo never ran for elected office but his facilities were popular with politicians who considered them "neutral territory." In 1962, an FBI wiretap caught a conversation between Philadelphia mob boss Angelo Bruno and another man in which it was implied the nightclub had a "safe" or "sterile" phone booth.

Palumbo was also a philanthropist who sent orphans to the circus and purchased animals for the Philadelphia Zoo. He once said, "If I stop giving, I stop living."

THIS USED TO BE: Palumbo's Cabaret

NOW IT'S: Rite-Aid Pharmacy

LOCATION: Bella Vista

Enjoying a Beverage while Bidding on Humans

In the early 1700s, the London Coffee House was the de facto meeting place for the city's most powerful people. Signers of the Declaration of Independence enjoyed beverages much stronger than coffee while planning the future of the nation. A merchant advertising his wares could enjoy a light meal called an "ordinary" while tucked in a private booth.

It was also where slave owners gathered as they waited for auctions of enslaved Africans and African Americans to begin. The humans sold stood on a small block outside the shop.

Slavery had been allowed in the colonies since 1684, when the British slave ship *Isabella* unloaded 150 captured Africans on docks a few blocks away. Even city founder William Penn, the devout Quaker who vowed all people were equal, owned slaves, although he probably called his forced laborers "servants" and stated they were "in service" as many others did.

The anti-slavery movement grew strong during the mid-1700s, supported by Founding Fathers Benjamin Franklin and Benjamin Rush. In 1780, Pennsylvania became the first colony to abolish slavery. Still, many remained in bondage. The last enslaved Pennsylvanian was freed in 1847.

On the northeast corner of Front and Market Streets is a statue honoring Chief Tamanend, the Lenni Lenape leader who welcomed William Penn in 1682. Tamanend means "the affable one" in the Lenni-Lenape language. Tamanend and Penn signed an accord promising that Quaker settlers and Native Americans would live side-by-side peacefully.

40

THE OLD LONDON COFFEE HOUSE, PHILADELPHIA.

may be entered on immediately.

TO BE SOLD,

On Saturday the 27th Inſtant, at the London Coffee-Houſe, TWELVE or Fourteen valuable NEGROES, confiſting of young Men, Women, Boys and Girls; they have all had the Small-Pox, can talk Engliſh, and are ſeaſoned to the Country. The Sale to begin at Twelve o'Clock.

SIX DOLLARS Reward.

RUN away, on the 19th Day of June laſt, from the Subſcri-

Located near the Delaware River, the London Coffee House was a hub of political activity and where enslaved Africans were bought and sold. (Image courtesy of the Free Library of Philadelphia.)

The London Coffee House was located at the corner of Front and High Street. High Street is now called Market Streets. (Image courtesy of the Library Company of Philadelphia.)

An 1891 article in *The Times* glosses over the selling of human beings, instead focusing on the other items auctioned here: "It was at 'the London,' in the year 1779, that the confiscated horses and chariot of the traitorous Benedict Arnold were sold under the hammer.... It was here, too, that the public sales were oftenest held, and among other goods and chattel disposed of were many slaves."

THIS USED TO BE: London Coffee House

NOW IT'S: Empty storefront

LOCATION: Old City

The Patriarch of a Long Line of Social Activists, Artists, and Intellectuals

Yes, Cyrus Bustill was a baker and the historic marker at 210 Arch Street acknowledges the bakery he and his family opened here in the late 1780s.

But he was much more than that. He cofounded the Free African Society, was an active member of the Underground Railroad, opened a school for African American children, and served as a church and civic leader whose descendants followed his lead in fighting for positive change.

Bustill was born enslaved in neighboring New Jersey in 1723; his father was the owner of the land where his mother was forced to live and work. He apprenticed with a New Jersey baker who taught Bustill the trade and allowed him to purchase his freedom. (One descendant later wrote that Bustill did not want "to perpetuate a race of slaves.")

Bustill was one of 5,000 freed Africans and African Americans who joined General George Washington's Continental Army, serving behind the lines. He provided bread to the future first president and his soldiers when they camped in Valley Forge.

A practicing Quaker, Bustill moved to Philadelphia after the war and quickly became a leader in the African American community. In 1787, with racial tensions in the city rising, Bustill addressed a large group of African Americans, telling them that nonviolent protest and presenting oneself as an equal was the best way to achieve emancipation, saying, "You being in bondage in particular, I would that ye take heed that afend

Civil Rights activist/actor Paul Robeson was the great-great-grandson of Cyrus and Elizabeth Bustill. The West Philadelphia home where Robeson lived in his final years, 4951 Walnut Street, is now a museum.

Fittingly, a pastry shop neighbors the property where Cyrus Bustill's bakery once stood. (Photo by Tricia Pompilio.)

(Romero, Rachael and Wilfred Owen Bridgade, Paul Robeson 1976, photograph. Retrieved from the Library of Congress, www.loc.gov/ item/96515950/.)

(offend) not with your tongue, be ye wise as Serpents and harmless as Doves, that he may take with you, when you are wrong'd."

Bustill and his wife, Elizabeth, ran the bakery with the help of their eight children. After retiring in 1797, he opened a school for African American children denied an education elsewhere. One of his daughters was the primary teacher.

The Bustills were one of the first prominent African American families in the United States and remain so today.

THIS USED TO BE: Cyrus Bustill's Bakery

NOW IT'S: Grossman Furniture Warehouse

LOCATION: Old City

At Long Last, a Dignified Resting Place

In September 2016, construction of a two-story subterranean parking garage came to an abrupt halt when workers uncovered human bones, broken grave markers and pieces of wood coffins. What started as a single banker's box of random bones gave way to a field full of graves.

The workers had uncovered a section of the First Baptist Church of Philadelphia's cemetery, one of the city's first burial grounds, founded here in 1707. When the church moved to a new location in the 1850s, its leaders arranged for the approximately 3,000 people interred here to be moved as well.

But some were left behind. Archeologists eventually uncovered the remains of about 500 people, including those who died during the yellow fever epidemics of 1793, 1797, and 1798. Three of the 500 were identified by name using clues from coffin plaques and headstones. One was Sarah M. Rogers, aged three years and nine months when she died in 1801. Another was Benjamin Britton, whose oversized and ornate coffin indicated that he'd been a very wealthy—and very large—man. All were moved and reinterred in another city cemetery.

In the years since the church was moved, the site had had multiple uses. It housed a felt hat factory until the late 1880s, a car repair shop in the mid-1900s, and a parking garage. Today it is a 10-story luxury apartment building, which in 2021 will begin offering "micro-units" starting at $1,275 per month, two-bedroom residences from $2,615, and underground parking spots for an extra cost.

Only three of the 500 graves found in the old First Baptist Church of Philadelphia cemetery were able to be identified. All remains were thought to have been moved in the 1850s. (Public domain, friendsofmountmoriahcemetery.org.)

The Betsy Ross House, across the road at 239-247 Arch Street, was the home and workshop of the creator of America's first flag.

· ·

THIS USED TO BE: First Baptist Church of Philadelphia Cemetery

NOW IT'S: Apartment Building

LOCATION: Old City

· ·

A Magazine for "Cultivators of the Soil"

In March 1877, Quaker journalist Wilmer Atkinson published the first edition of *Farm Journal*, a magazine he promised would "possess real value to the class for whom it is published—the cultivators of the soil—and an entertaining monthly visitor to rural firesides.... The future will determine the measure of our success." The periodical was so popular that it was produced from here for 139 years, an irony the *Philadelphia Inquirer* noted when an article to mark the journal's 125th anniversary noted that the "Magazine speaks to the farmer from offices in urban Philadelphia."

Atkinson printed 25,000 copies of his first edition, selling each for twenty-five cents and sending them out for delivery via horseback to farms within a day's ride of the city. In an introductory letter, Atkinson promised the journal would not contain "lottery swindles, cheap jewelry advertisements, [or] quack medical advertisements." Instead, it would be "practical, not fancy" farming. That inaugural edition had articles on the care of shade trees, the use of glass frames to protect baby chicks born in February and March, and tips on strawberry growing and sheep raising.

Readership grew steadily, reaching a nationwide audience of one million in 1915 and a peak of 3.7 million in 1953. The Philadelphia office eventually grew to include radio and television broadcasting studios.

Pennsylvania Hospital is the nation's first hospital. It offers tours that include Thomas Eakins's *The Gross Clinic* and the surgical theater featured in the painting.

The *Farm Journal* was published in downtown Philadelphia for more than a century. The building is now part of Pennsylvania Hospital. (Photo by Tricia Pompilio.)

The first edition of the *Farm Journal* was published in 1877. About 250,000 copies were sold for 25 cents each. (Public domain, pinterest.com.)

THIS USED TO BE: Farm Journal Building

NOW IT'S: Pennsylvania Hospital Offices

LOCATION: Washington Square

The Original *Mad Men*

In 1869, Francis Ayer opened the country's first advertising firm, N.W. Ayer & Son. Over the next century, it would create some of the world's best-known slogans, including "Diamonds Are Forever" for the DeBeers mining syndicate; "Be All You Can Be" for the US Army; and "Reach Out and Touch Someone" for AT&T's long-distance service.

Ayer changed the advertising industry, building a close relationship with its clients instead of being mere middlemen selling newsprint space. As the 1900s dawned, Ayer was on top of its game: in 1913, R.J. Reynolds hired Ayer to promote the new Camel cigarette, reportedly saying that the country's best tobacco company deserved the country's best advertising firm. Reynolds reportedly paid the company $250,000 (about $6.6 million in today's dolllars) to launch its new product.

Ayer created four different ads for Camels, publishing each on a full newspaper page one day after the other. Consumers were hooked: more than 450 million Camel cigarettes were sold that year, making R.J. Reynolds one of the "Big Three" tobacco companies. Other Camel ads by Ayer include "No better cigarette can be made" and "The Camels are coming." News anchor Edward R. Murrow was often pictured smoking an unfiltered Camel.

Not long after that success, the company built this Art Deco building on Washington Square. Its ornate checkerboard door features reliefs meant to honor those in the print industry, including a figure holding a painter's palette, people working at a printing press, and someone writing a manuscript.

Washington Square is one of the city's five original green spaces. At one point it served as a graveyard for Revolutionary War soldiers, which is why there is a statue for General George Washington and an eternal flame on one side of the park.

Ayer created some of the best known advertisements of the twentieth century. (Public domain, intheweeds.bandcamp.com.)

Ayer's successful Camel campaign helped R.J. Reynolds become one of the "Big Three" in the tobacco industry. (Public domain, camelbrand.wordpress.com.)

The Ayer company moved to New York and continued to excel until the 1960s. It gradually lost ground to newer advertising companies and merged with other agencies. Its last owner retired the Ayer name in 2002. Today the ad agency's former headquarters is a luxury condominium complex called The Ayer.

THIS USED TO BE: N.W. Ayer & Son Advertising

NOW IT'S: The Ayer—Condominiums

LOCATION: Washington Square

The Athens of America

Before the Philadelphia Bourse commodities exchange brought the city's businessmen together, individual industries ran their own, smaller exchanges. In 1831, Stephen Girard, the country's richest man, led efforts to build the Merchants' Exchange Building, now a popular city landmark.

Philadelphia was thriving in post–Revolutionary War America, a hub of business and industry, culture and learning. The city had been dubbed "the Athens of America" in the 1700s because of its Greek name and its role in the establishment of American democracy. In the early 1800s, Philadelphia began to physically resemble the Greek city, too, as a fervor for Greek Revival–style architecture grew. Noted architect Benjamin Latrobe mused that the "days of Greece may be revived in the woods of America."

The architect chosen to design the Merchants' Exchange was William Strickland, a one-time student of Latrobe's. Strickland said his design blended elements of two landmarks in the Greek capital: the Choragic Monument of Lysicrates and the Tower of the Winds. The facades on the east and west sides are completely different, yet are brought together via marble Corinthian columns.

Merchants' Exchange replaced nearby City Tavern, 138 South 2nd Street, as a business hub. The original tavern building was destroyed by fire in the 1830s. In the 1970s, a historically accurate replica was built in its place. Before it shut down in late 2020, the restaurant offered a menu of eighteenth-century-inspired cuisine, including West Indies pepperpot soup and turkey pot pie.

The Greek Revival Merchants' Exchange was built on the idea of Philadelphia as the Athens of America. (Image courtesy of Library Company of Philadelphia.)

The poet George Webb wrote:

Stretch'd on the Bank of Delaware's rapid Stream
Stands Philadelphia, not unknown to Fame;
Here the tall Vessels safe at Anchor ride,
And Europe's Wealth flows in with every Tide
Who (if the wishing Muse inspir'd does sing)
Shall Liberal arts to such Perfection bring,
Europe shall mourn her ancient Fame declin'd
And Philadelphia be the Athens of Mankind.

THIS USED TO BE: Merchants' Exchange

NOW IT'S: National Park Service Offices

LOCATION: Old City

Buy, Sell, Ship via Philadelphia

The Philadelphia Bourse was the first commodities center in the United States, putting a stock exchange, maritime exchange, and grain-training center together under one roof. Founded in 1891, the Bourse moved into this Beaux-Arts building four years later.

Local businessman George E. Bartol was inspired to create the Philadelphia Bourse after visiting a similar institution in Hamburg, Germany. An 1895 *Philadelphia Inquirer* article described the German business hub: "The commercial interests of Hamburg are united in a single body which is able to act with precision, swiftness and force, upon any matter affecting them. Hamburg has always had large commercial importance, and possibly the secret of its success in this direction lies in the combination of business men for the promotion of their interests."

Each member of the Bourse contributed $1,000 to the project. The Bourse motto was "Buy, Sell, Ship via Philadelphia."

The Bourse was a business center for the city until the 1960s. In 2018, its private owners closed most of the building for a $40 million renovation, which uncovered original details including tile from 1895. The upper floors house offices, including the Mexican consulate. The lower floors hold retail shops and a food court.

The Bourse is located in the heart of Independence Mall. After a day of touring, stop here for lunch. It has 30 food vendors with offerings that range from Filipino comfort food to Hawaiian Poke to Korean Tacos.

The Philadelphia Bourse was the first commodities center in the United States. It was inspired by a similar facility in Hamburg, Germany. (Detroit Publishing Co., Philadelphia Bourse, Philadelphia, Pa. Photograph. Retrieved from the Library of Congress, www.loc.gov/item/2016799740/.)

Today the building houses offices, retail, and restaurants. (Photo by Tricia Pompilio.)

THIS USED TO BE: The Bourse, the country's first commodities center

NOW IT'S: The Bourse, a multiuse property with retail, restaurants, and offices

LOCATION: Independence Mall Historic District

A Shot for Commerce

Built in 1808, the Sparks Shot Tower was the first of its kind in the United States. It made musket ammunition and birdshot by pouring hot lead through a mesh screen near the top of the tower. (The size of the holes in the screen determined the size of the finished product.) When the lead hit a vat holding six feet of water more than 140 feet below, it formed a ball. That technique proved much cheaper and faster than pouring lead into wooden molds.

In 1891, *The Times Sunday* ran an article headlined "By A Secret Process: How Lead is Turned into Instruments of Destruction; Work in a Big Shot Tower," noting it was unlikely that "not one of the thousands who use it, from the sportsman who fires the little leaden pellets to bring down his game, to the thrifty housewife who uses it to clean her bottles, knows of the ingenious methods employed in turning the pig lead into the shot of commerce."

Thomas Sparks and his business partners sold military munitions during the War of 1812 and the Civil War. The Sparks family eventually took over the business, with four generations managing operations until 1903. The city purchased the tower and the surrounding grounds a decade later and turned it into a recreation center.

The Shot Tower's outdoor playground is open to the public.

Built in 1808, the Sparks Shot Tower was the first of its kind in the United States. (Public domain, pinterest.com.)

This more recent photo of the Sparks Shot Tower shows it as it looks today, with sports field lighting and a recreation center. (Public domain, Library of Congress via atlasobscura.com.)

THIS USED TO BE: Sparks Shot Tower

NOW IT'S: Shot Tower Recreation Center

LOCATION: Queen Village

Freedom, Slavery, and the First White House

Presidents George Washington and John Quincy Adams lived and governed from the house that stood here for the 10 years Philadelphia was the nation's capital. Washington called the three-story brick structure "the best single house in the city."

When the Redcoats captured the city during the Revolutionary War, British General Sir William Hall used the home as his headquarters. Other occupants included Benedict Arnold and financier Robert Morris, who gifted the property to Washington. When the nation's capital moved to DC, the house became a hotel, then a hardware store, and later a general department store.

What remained of the building was demolished in the 1950s when the National Park Service created Independence Mall. The "first White House" was largely forgotten until 2000, when construction of a new Liberty Bell pavilion began. The excavation uncovered the home's original kitchen and root cellar and the two-story state dining room which featured a bow window that inspired the shape of the Oval Office.

This painting attributed to Gilbert Stuart, *Presumed Portrait of George Washington's Cook*, is thought to depict Hercules, the enslaved African who cooked for the Washington family. (Public domain, ushistory.org.)

One exhibit on the open-air footprint of the original dwelling is *The President's House: Freedom and Slavery in the Making of a New Nation*. Nine enslaved persons of African descent served the Washington household. America's first president had no interest in abolition. He skirted a Philadelphia law that would have freed his workers after six months of city occupancy by sending them on day trips across the Delaware River to New Jersey.

Oney Judge and Hercules were two of the Washingtons' servants. Oney was Martha Washington's personal maid while Hercules was a gifted chef. Both escaped, which shocked and angered Washington, who thought he'd given them a privileged life.

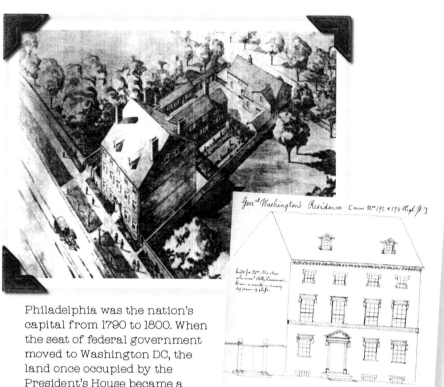

Philadelphia was the nation's capital from 1790 to 1800. When the seat of federal government moved to Washington DC, the land once occupied by the President's House became a hotel, a hardware store and a department store before being torn down in the 1960s. ("Residence of Washington in High Street, Philada." by William L. Breton. Public domain, wikipedia.org.)

The President's House had a bowed window that inspired the shape of the Oval Office when the nation's capital moved to Washington, DC. (Image courtesy of the Library Company of Philadelphia.)

Abolitionists adopted the Liberty Bell as a symbol of their movement. The bell's history is written on the outside walls of the pavilion in which it sits.

THIS USED TO BE: President's House

NOW IT'S: Historic Landmark

LOCATION: Independence Mall Historic District

Thanks for the Thin Mints!

"Twenty-three cents a box—six boxes for $1.35. A treat for one week. Hurry!"

Thank the Girl Scouts of Greater Philadelphia for that box of Thin Mints hidden in the back of the freezer. In the 1930s, the council launched a cookie baking and selling fundraiser that was the precursor of the one still in use today.

Juliette Gordon Low founded the Girl Scouts in 1912. Individual troops baked and sold cookies as early as 1915. The main organization encouraged such entrepreneurship. In the 1920s, the official Girl Scout magazine published a sugar cookie recipe, noting that seven dozen cookies would cost about thirty-five cents to produce. The girls were encouraged to sell the cookies door to door, at between twenty-five and thirty cents per dozen.

When the stock market crashed in 1929, the organization urged its 250,000 young members to help others. Soon after, a Philadelphia Scout told her parents she wanted to bake cookies to distribute to children in need. She and her fellow Scouts were able to use demonstration ovens at Philadelphia Gas and Electric company. After distributing cookies throughout the city, the Scouts sold the extras to passers-by who'd followed their noses to the PG&E storefront. The company was so pleased with the publicity that it allowed the Scouts to use their ovens the following year as well.

In 1934, Philadelphia Scout leaders hired the Keebler-Weyl Baking Company near Logan Square to produce 100,000 boxes of vanilla cookies shaped like the Girl Scouts' trefoil symbol. Impressed, the national organization decided to follow suit, launching the first nationwide cookie sale in 1936.

Thin Mints, the Scouts' most popular variety, debuted in 1939. Today, the Girl Scouts sell about 200 million boxes annually, with all proceeds funding Scout activities.

First Lady Grace Coolidge tries a cookie in 1923. The three women around her are Girl Scout Troop leaders. (Mrs. Coolidge eating cookies presented by a New York Girl Scout Troop. Photograph. Retrieved from the Library of Congress, www.loc.gov/item/2002712383/.)

A Girl Scout serves cookies. (Harris & Ewing, photographer. Photograph. Retrieved from the Library of Congress, www.loc.gov/item/2016882225/.)

City Hall, 1400 JFK Boulevard, is one block from the former bakery site. The grounds around the building offer ice-skating in winter and a sprayground in summer.

THIS USED TO BE: Keebler-Weyl Baking Company

NOW IT'S: Office building with empty first floor retail

LOCATION: Center City

A Beloved Stooge's Birthplace

Louis Feinberg—later known as Larry Fine—was born in the house that stood here in 1902. In 1928, he joined the Howard brothers as one of the Three Stooges. He would perform as the "middle Stooge" until illness abruptly ended his career in 1970.

Fine was the oldest of four children born to Russian Jewish parents who ran a jewelry and watch store. A mural on the wall of his birthplace shows him playing the violin as he did in many Stooge skits. Fine took up the instrument after accidentally spilling corrosive acid on his left arm. Doctors suggested the boy take lessons to rebuild his damaged muscles.

Fine was a natural musician. At age nine, he performed with the Philadelphia Orchestra and his music teacher saw a career for him as a concert violinist. His parents planned to send him to a European music conservatory until World War I quashed that plan.

In his late teens, Fine worked as an underwear salesman while developing a Vaudeville-style act. He joined forces with fellow Stooges/brothers Moe and Curly Howard in the 1930s, starring in more than 200 short and feature films.

Fine's high school, Central, inducted him into its Hall of Fame even though it's believed he did not graduate. A 2009 *Philadelphia Inquirer* article about the induction called Fine "the poodle-haired Nyuk Nyuk Nyuk" with one Central organizer noting that "Larry Fine's probably had more of an impact on generations than anybody."

The Stoogeum, a museum of Stooges memorabilia, is located in Spring House, a 35-minute drive from Philadelphia.

Larry Fine began playing violin to strengthen his arm after an accident. (Photo by Tricia Pompilio.)

Curly Howard, Larry Fine, and Moe Howard performed together as "The Three Stooges" for almost 50 years. (Public domain, wikipedia.org.)

THIS USED TO BE: Home of Larry Fine

NOW IT'S: Empty restaurant space

LOCATION: Queen Village

A Legendary Chocolatier's Not-So-Sweet Beginnings

Milton Snavely Hershey was 18 when he borrowed $150 and opened his first candy store, M.S. Hershey, Wholesale and Retail Confectioner, at this location in June 1876.

Hershey, from rural Lebanon Valley, PA, had ended his formal education after fourth grade. He spent four years apprenticing with a local candy maker before deciding to go out on his own. He chose to set up shop in Philadelphia, about 65 miles to the east, so as not to compete with his former teacher and to take advantage of the crowds visiting the city's Centennial International Exhibition, the first official World's Fair held in the United States.

Hershey initially worked alone, making caramels and taffy into the early morning hours, sometimes sleeping on the store's counter. Come daylight he'd load his fresh candy onto a pushcart and walk to the fairgrounds to sell his wares. He used a sketch of one of the fair's buildings on his official business card.

Hershey's store initially turned a small profit. But business slowed when the Fair ended that November. To attract customers to his store, Hershey installed a pipe to carry the sweet scents rising from his kettles into the surrounding neighborhood. Hershey's mother and aunt moved to Philadelphia to assist him at the store, but it never gained its footing. The shop closed in 1882.

After three more failed businesses, Hershey found his sweet spot: Inspired by a trip to Switzerland, one of the world's largest producers of finished chocolate, he began experimenting with milk chocolate recipes. He introduced the first American candy bar—the Hershey bar—in 1900. The factory he opened to produce it would go on to become the world's

Hersheypark, the amusement park owned by Hershey, is a less than two-hour drive from Philadelphia.

Three Big Sellers

Printed in SILVER INK on distinctive HERSHEY MAROON labels.

"More Sustaining than Meat" was the motto on the wrapper of this Hershey's Sweet Milk Chocolate bar from the early 1900s. (Public domain, pinterest.com.)

Milton Hershey refused to let his failure in Philadelphia stop him from launching a chocolate empire. He was continually developing new products, including a chocolate bar with almonds and a hot cocoa mix.(Courtesy of the Hershey Community Archives.)

Milton S. Hershey, seen here in 1887 at age 30, built an entire town to support his growing candy factories. (Public domain, pinterest.com.)

largest chocolate-manufacturing plant. In fact, Hershey would eventually build an entire town to house his many workers. Today, Hershey, PA, is also called Chocolate Town, USA, with streets bearing names like Cocoa and Chocolate and downtown streetlights shaped like the company's signature Kisses.

THIS USED TO BE: Milton Hershey's First Candy Store

NOW IT'S: Empty storefront

LOCATION: Callowhill

Philadelphia's Princess

In the 1920s, three-time Olympic gold medalist turned successful businessman John B. Kelly Sr. designed and built a Georgian brick home in the East Falls neighborhood for his growing family. Among his brood: John B. Kelly Jr., a four-time Olympian and past president of the US Olympics Foundation, and Academy Award–winning actress Grace Kelly, who later became the Princess of Monaco.

The young movie star was a favorite of director Alfred Hitchcock, who featured her in three of his films: *Dial M for Murder*, *Rear Window*, and *To Catch a Thief*. She acted opposite some of the most famous male stars of the age, including Gary Cooper and Cary Grant. Hitchcock was reportedly infatuated with the actress, which was understandable according to one of her costars, James Stewart. "How could Hitch not help but fall in love with Grace? Everyone loved her," said Stewart.

Kelly won her Best Actress Oscar in 1955 for *The Country Girl*. That same year, a friend told her that Prince Rainier III wanted to meet her. Kelly balked. "I'd be bored," she said. Still, she agreed to the meeting. Rainier proposed less than a year later with a Cartier band studded with diamonds and rubies representing the colors of Monaco.

A 1956 Associated Press article datelined Hollywood began: "This movie town, which loves the Cinderella story, couldn't be more pleased that Grace Kelly is engaged to the Prince of Monaco. Or surprised. The news was the biggest bombshell to hit the town since Marilyn left Joe."

The Kelly family sold their Philadelphia house in the 1970s. Subsequent owners allowed it to fall into disrepair. Kelly died unexpectedly in a car accident in 1982 at age 52.

In 2016, Kelly's son, Prince Albert II of Monaco, purchased the property for $754,000. He spent two years renovating it to look as it did

Kelly Drive, which runs along the Schuylkill River, is named after Grace Kelly's brother, John B. Kelly Jr., a city councilman. A statue of her father, Olympic gold medalist John B. Kelly Sr., is near Boathouse Row.

This paneled room in the childhood home of actress Grace Kelly is said to be little changed today. (Public domain, pinterest.com.)

Actress Grace Kelly's childhood home is now owned by her son, Prince Albert II of Monaco. (Zach Pagano/TODAY.)

when his mother lived there, using family photos and videos for clues. The second-floor linen closet door is still marked with the heights of the four Kelly children from ages two until their teens. The wood-paneled room where Kelly and Rainier held their post-engagement press conference is little changed.

The home is now the American headquarters for the offices of the Prince Albert II of Monaco Foundation, a nonprofit dedicated to environmental protection. The prince and his family stay here when visiting the United States.

THIS USED TO BE: Home of Grace Kelly

NOW IT'S: Offices of the Prince Albert II of Monaco Foundation and Royal Residence

LOCATION: East Falls

Seeking a Seat at the Counter

In 1965, 150 protestors took seats inside the Dewey's restaurant which stood here and refused to leave until management stopped discriminating against lesbian, gay, bisexual, transgender, and queer diners. After a second sit-in and five days of protests outside the diner, Dewey's management agreed to serve all patrons. It was one of the LGBTQ community's first wins in its fight for equality and it took place four years before New York's Stonewall Inn uprising.

Dewey's was a popular regional chain known for its malted milkshakes, burgers, and hot dogs. In the 1960s, the restaurant on South 13th Street was known as the Gay Dewey's, an all-night venue located in the heart of what is now the Gayborhood. Another area Dewey's, about five blocks away at South 17th and Latimer Streets, was also becoming popular with the LGBTQ community.

Managers of the South 17th Street restaurant weren't happy about that. In April 1965, they told servers to not take orders from anyone who they believed to be homosexual or wearing clothing they considered outside the mainstream. The pushback was immediate: 150 patrons who were denied service refused to leave. Police broke up the sit-in, arresting four people for disorderly conduct.

In the days that followed, protesters marched up and down the sidewalk in front of the restaurant and held another sit-in on May 2. Police on the scene declined to make arrests. Soon after the protest, the management rescinded its discriminatory policy.

Rittenhouse Square, one of the city's five original green spaces, is less than a block away across Walnut Street.

The 1965 sit-in at Dewey's restaurant was one of the earliest LGBTQ rights protests in the United States. (Public domain, pinterest.com.)

After three teenagers were arrested on the first day of the protest, members of an LGBTQ rights group handed out 1,500 educational pamphlets for five days before staging a second sit-in. (Photo courtesy of the John J. Wilcox Jr. LGBT Archives at the William Way Community Center.)

THIS USED TO BE: Dewey's Restaurant

NOW IT'S: Private residence

LOCATION: Center City

A Shakespearean Riot

Edwin Forrest, who lived here until his death in 1872, was one of the best-known actors of his time, a thespian who could list Abraham Lincoln as one of his biggest fans. Today, Forrest is known not only for his stage accomplishments but also for his role in 1849's Astor Place Riot.

Forrest was the first US-born actor to find a following here and abroad as American theater was still dominated by the Brits. Forrest developed a rivalry with British star William Macready. Fans of each actor would openly argue over which was the best interpreter of Shakespeare.

In 1849, both men were performing *Hamlet* in New York theaters. As Macready waited to take the stage one night, Forrest fans in the audience began booing and hissing, throwing tomatoes and eggs. The show was canceled.

On the night of the rescheduled performance, police officers surrounded the theater, watching as an uneasy crowd of about 10,000 people—a mixture of Forrest fans and Macready supporters—steadily grew. When Macready took the stage, Forrest fans rushed the building, but were beaten back by club-wielding cops. As the brawl continued, city leaders called a nearby company of soldiers to aid the police. The rioters attacked the militia with bricks. In response, the soldiers opened fire.

At least 20—and perhaps as many as 40 —people were killed. Scores more were injured.

An 11-foot-tall statue of Forrest stands inside the Walnut Street Theatre, 825 Walnut Street, where Forrest made his acting debut in 1820 at age 14. Three blocks east is the Forrest Theatre, 1114 Walnut Street, which the Schubert brothers opened in 1928 and named to honor Forrest.

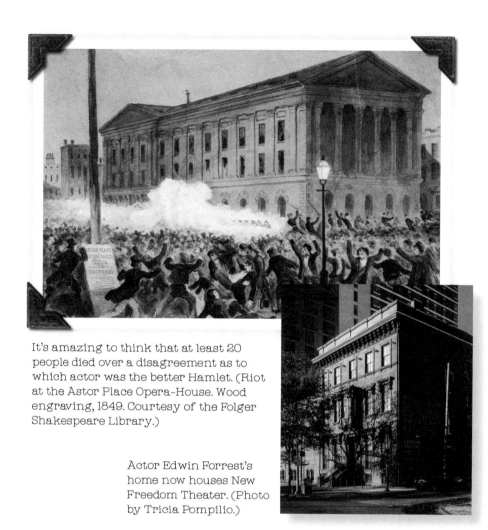

It's amazing to think that at least 20 people died over a disagreement as to which actor was the better Hamlet. (Riot at the Astor Place Opera-House. Wood engraving, 1849. Courtesy of the Folger Shakespeare Library.)

Actor Edwin Forrest's home now houses New Freedom Theater. (Photo by Tricia Pompilio.)

THIS USED TO BE: Home of Edwin Forrest

NOW IT'S: New Freedom Theater

LOCATION: Lower North Philadelphia

An Inn with "A View to Delight a Poet"

By late 1870, wealthy industrialist Henry Howard Houston had had enough of Philadelphia's dirty, crowded downtown. He purchased 2,000 acres about 11 miles away from Center City, building a home for himself and an opulent hotel for those who could afford to stay there. To further ensure success, Houston used his influence as a former Pennsylvania Railroad executive to add a regional rail stop outside the hotel's front door.

The Wissahickon Inn, an opulent 250-room resort with views of the Wissahickon Valley, opened in 1884. An article in the *Philadelphia Inquirer* praised the hotel's "architectural beauty and interior elegance" and described its surroundings as "a view to delight a poet."

The resort was an immediate success, drawing patrons from across the United States and Canada. Houston donated adjacent land to the Philadelphia Cricket Club, which expanded to offer tennis and golf. In 1892, the Inn hosted the first Philadelphia Horse Show, drawing more than 10,000 guests.

Houston had an estimated wealth of $15 million—about $470 million today—with investments in California and Nevada gold mines, Colorado silver mines, and the growing oil industry. He aimed to give away 10 percent of his income each year to charities. When he died in 1895, his obituary in the Wilkes-Barre *Union-Leader* noted, "He was known for his philanthropy but many of his beneficence acts are unknown. He gave with free hand to every deserving object that was presented to him and none ever appealed to him in vain."

In 1898, the Chestnut Hill Academy, an all-boys pre-K to 12 college prep school, began using the inn during the off-season. The school moved here full-time three years later.

Houston's home, Druim Moir Castle, Willow Grove Avenue and Cherokee Street, was completed in 1886. The original structure had 30 rooms and stood on a 55-acre plot.

The lavish Wissahickon Inn was a three-story hotel featuring gables and dormers, a wrap-around porch, and a glass-enclosed dining room. (Historic American Buildings Survey, Creator. Wissahickon Inn ... Retrieved from Library of Congress, www.loc.gov/item/pa1364/)

Henry H. Houston was a philanthropist who in 1879 donated $100,000 to build Houston Hall on the campus of the University of Pennsylvania. (Public Domain, wikipedia.org.)

THIS USED TO BE: Wissahickon Inn

NOW IT'S: Springside Chestnut Hill Academy

LOCATION: Chestnut Hill

Eliminating Suffering Fueled by "Ignorance and Destitution"

Doctor/politician/banker/shipping magnate Jonas Preston always found time to volunteer, providing medical care to the indigent. When he died in 1835, his will decreed that half of his fortune—$200,000, or about $5.9 million today—go toward the construction of a "Lying-In-Hospital . . . for Indigent Married Females of good character, distinct and unconnected with any other Hospital." The facility was needed, Preston's will said, because "I have no doubt there is often much suffering and loss of life in such cases, from the effects of ignorance and destitution."

Preston Retreat, located in a handsome Greek Revival style building, began welcoming patients in 1865. The women attended a 20-week-long prenatal clinic that not only monitored their pregnancies but also sent them home with "milk, vitamin tonics or other medicines—even coal to warm her house" if needed, the hospital's guidelines showed.

The expectant mothers moved into the hospital a week before their due dates and were allowed to stay for two weeks afterward. They were given clean clothes, all meals, and two baths per week. One of the most remarkable things about the hospital was its infant mortality rate. At a time when the nationwide rate was 10 percent, the Preston Retreat rate was .09 percent.

Preston Retreat also provided hands-on training to students from Pennsylvania Hospital's School of Nursing. When the building was torn down in the 1960s, Pennsylvania Hospital absorbed its services and in 1971 opened the Preston Building.

Walk around the area to see the few remaining Greek columns on the property.

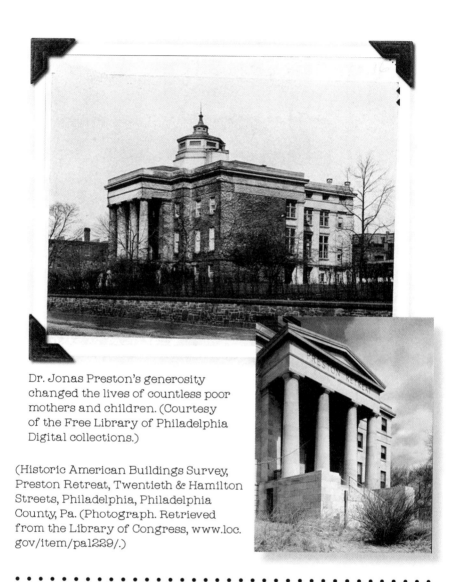

Dr. Jonas Preston's generosity changed the lives of countless poor mothers and children. (Courtesy of the Free Library of Philadelphia Digital collections.)

(Historic American Buildings Survey, Preston Retreat, Twentieth & Hamilton Streets, Philadelphia, Philadelphia County, Pa. (Photograph. Retrieved from the Library of Congress, www.loc.gov/item/pa1229/.)

THIS USED TO BE: Preston Retreat

NOW IT'S: CityView — Condominiums

LOCATION: Franklintown

As Important to Basketball as the Actual Ball

For three decades, the South Philadelphia Hebrew Association basketball team—the SPHAs (pronounced "spahs")—dominated East Coast basketball, playing in multiple leagues and winning 12 championships. In the 1920s and 30s, the team played its Saturday night home games in the grand ballroom of the Broadwood Hotel, which stood here until the 1990s.

Eddie Gottlieb, who later coached in the NBA, cofounded the SPHAs in 1918. The team's name, written in Hebrew on the front of players' "Jewish blue" jerseys, came from one of its earliest and biggest sponsors. Fittingly, most of its players were Jewish and the team was nicknamed The Wandering Jews before it settled at the Broadwood in the 1930s. It hosted American Basketball League teams including the Bronx Americans, the Camden Electrics, and the Trenton Moose.

The SPHAs cared about more than winning games, as Gottlieb noted in an interview with the Associated Press: "We played in a lot of dance halls in those early years. It was basketball, then dancing... We used to let the girls in for free, because you couldn't have a dance after the game without the girls. We had no trouble getting the guys to pay for the basketball game when they heard that."

In 1946, team owners across the country formed the 11-team Basketball Association of America. Gottlieb became the owner and head coach of the Philadelphia Warriors, which won the league's first championship. Three years later, the Basketball Association of America merged with the National Basketball League, creating today's NBA.

Gottlieb graduated from South Philadelphia High School in 1916. A historic plaque in front of the school at 2101 South Broad Street acknowledges some of his contributions to the game of basketball.

A 1940 photo of the Philadelphia SPHAs players, coaches, and staff. (Photo courtesy of Special Collections Research Center, Temple University Libraries.)

Gottlieb still owned the Warriors when the team won the 1956 NBA championship.

Gottlieb, whose nicknames included "The Mogul" and "Mr. Basketball," took a job in the NBA's front offices, leading its rules committee for 25 years and making its schedules for almost 30 years. To do this, a 2014 *Philadelphia Inquirer* article said, "He wrote out the schedule on paper napkins in restaurants or jotted down notes on a pad he kept by his bedside. In his head, Gottlieb kept track of train schedules and holidays that could disrupt his planning."

When Gottlieb died in 1979, Basketball Hall of Famer Harry Litwack said, "Gottlieb was about as important to the game of basketball as the basketball."

The Broadwood, which had been an Elks Lodge before being converted to a hotel, later became the Philadelphia Sports Club. It was razed to build a parking garage for nearby Hahnemann Hospital.

THIS USED TO BE: Home Court of the SPHAs Basketball Team

NOW IT'S: Parking Garage

LOCATION: Lower North Philadelphia

The Plexiglas Palace

While chemical giant Rohm and Haas left the city in 2016, its former downtown headquarters remains a tribute to the company and its most iconic product: Plexiglas.

Chemist Otto Rohm and businessman Otto Haas founded their eponymous company in Germany in the early 1900s. Rohm spent about a decade perfecting the formula for the hard, transparent, shatterproof acrylic. In the 1930s, the company trademarked the name *Plexiglas* and began producing sheets for commercial production. In 1937, the company won a gold medal at the Paris World's Fair for its translucent violin made of Plexiglas.

Plexiglas was used for airplane cockpits and turrets during World War II. Its peacetime applications include bank teller windows, protective partitions in hockey rinks, signs, taillights, eyeglasses, skylights, light fixtures, and lawn furniture.

In the late 1950s, as Philadelphia leaders were reimagining the area around Independence Hall, Rohm and Haas purchased this property. It had one rule for its architects and contractors: incorporate Plexiglas into the final design.

The completed Rohm and Haas building, a $10 million, nine-story, mid-century modern, concrete structure covered in bronze Plexiglas sunscreens, opened in the mid-1960s. The interior features Plexiglas chandeliers, light fixtures, walls, and windows. One architecture critic said the structure "was probably the most handsome building in Philadelphia."

Dow Chemical purchased Rohm and Haas in 2009. The company moved out of the city about eight years later.

Get closer to the building and enjoy food and drink at Independence Beer Garden, the 20,000-square-foot outdoor space that can accommodate 300 guests.

The Rohm and Haas is one of the best examples of
the international style that defined mid-twentieth-
century architecture. (Photo by Tricia Pompilio.)

THIS USED TO BE: Rohm and Haas Corporate
Headquarters

NOW IT'S: Office building with restaurant space

LOCATION: Independence Mall Historic District

From Funeral Home to Clothing Monument

In 1907, undertaker Oliver H. Bair built this stately five-story building to house his growing business, infusing it with a sense of lushness by using white marble, decorative columns, bronze busts, and a double grand staircase that led to an enormous organ. Bair had no way of knowing that, decades later, his space would be occupied by a store which sells individual men's suits more costly than a full funeral, including coffin and internment, in his day.

Bair opened his first Philadelphia funeral home in 1878. Business grew rapidly. At its peak, the company employed 85 people and hosted more than 2,000 funerals annually.

When Bair purchased the land at 1818-20 Chestnut Street, he wanted a building that would impress and also convey a message: You and your loved ones are worth the best. That said, he was also very much a man of the people. His company's slogan, "No Deserving Poor Refused," appeared on placards posted on trolleys and buses. He was one of the first undertakers to offer pre-need financing, allowing people to pay ten or fifteen cents per week to finance their future funerals. A 1900 *Philadelphia Inquirer* article said that thanks to Bair's payment program, "First class funerals are placed in the reach of all."

Bair wanted to be more than a casket salesman. He wanted to care for people. He stressed customer service, offering grieving families temporary apartments, private mourning rooms, and the proverbial shoulder to cry on. His employees shared his commitment to being "Philadelphia's finest funeral directors." Some spent their entire careers—40, even 50 years—with Bair.

Business slowed in the 1980s and the company moved the bulk of its operation to the suburbs. Boyd's, a high-end clothing company that specializes in custom-made garments, moved into the building in 1990. Its staff includes more than 25 tailors.

OLIVER H. BAIR, FOUNDER

Oliver Bair was a funeral industry pioneer who worked to ensure everyone could have a decent farewell. (Images courtesy of the Oliver H. Bair Co. & Monaghan Funeral Home.)

Boyd's interior is something to behold and it's well worth going inside the store.

THIS USED TO BE: Oliver H. Bair Funeral Home

NOW IT'S: Boyd's Philadelphia

LOCATION: Center City

The Business That Birthed a Neighborhood

As anti-Chinese sentiment continued to grow on the West Coast in the late 1860s, an immigrant named Lee Fong headed east. When he arrived in Philadelphia in 1871, he opened a laundry service at 913 Race Street. His was the city's first Chinese-owned business, a cornerstone of Philadelphia's modern Chinatown.

Less than a decade later, Fong's cousin opened the city's first Chinese restaurant, Mei-Hsian Lou, on the second floor of the same building. As the years passed, more Chinese-owned businesses grew outward from the corner of 9th and Race Streets. Most of the immigrants were men who had been forced to leave their wives and children in China. Together they formed "bachelor societies."

Laundries were popular starter businesses for Chinese immigrants because the work required no special skills or start-up money. Hand-washing clothes was also an undesirable job requiring long days standing over vats of boiling water and hours removing wrinkles with an iron heated on a stove top. Fong opened his shop close to the city's docks, so it would be easy for workers to drop off their clothing.

Today, a painted mural a few blocks from Fong's original building, *History of Chinatown*, acknowledges his role in the birth of the neighborhood. A laundry worker is depicted top center, wringing fabric by hand, the falling drops of water forming a river and roads. The number 913 is near the mural's center.

Philadelphia has the third largest Chinatown on the East Coast, home to about 3,000 people. The vast majority of residents are of Asian descent. It's a close-knit group; they say if you bring any 20 residents together, at least five will be related.

The colorful "Friendship Gate," Arch and North 10th Streets, is the unofficial entrance to the neighborhood. It was installed here in 1984 by artists from Philadelphia's sister city, Tianjin.

Lee Fong is painted at the top of this mural, wringing laundry and allowing the water to spill downward and create the Chinatown neighborhood. (Highsmith, Carol M., photographer. History of Chinatown mural, by four artists "Arturo Ho, Giz, N. Phung, and H. Tran. Philadelphia, Pennsylvania. Photograph. Retrieved from the Library of Congress, www.loc.gov/item/2019689264/.)

In 1984, artists from Tianjin, China, came to Philadelphia to help build Chinatown's "Friendship Gate." Tianjin is one of Philadelphia's sister cities. (Photo by G. Widman for VISIT PHILADELPHIA.)

THIS USED TO BE: Lee Fong Laundry

NOW IT'S: Empty storefront

LOCATION: Chinatown

A Radio Headquarters Like No Other

By the late 1920s it was clear that radio was more than a passing fad. That's why the owners of WCAU built this state-of-the-art broadcasting facility in 1931. It was the first building in the United States specifically constructed as a radio station headquarters.

WCAU, a CBS-affiliated station, had launched in 1922 in the back of an electrician's shop. Philadelphia was a hub for the blossoming industry. An article in the 1927 *Wilmington (DE) Evening Journal* noted the city's connection with the electrical industry "started with Franklin's famous experiment with the key and kite . . . the first storage batteries used by Marconi were furnished by a Philadelphia organization, and that the largest output of storage batteries in the world is manufactured in this city."

The building remains one of the city's finest examples of Art Deco architecture. Its shiny blue facade, then and now, has a futuristic feel with metal accents in chrome, copper, and brass. Some of the silver accents seem a nod to the building's original purpose, with jagged lightning bolts emanating from a central rectangle as sound waves would soar into the air from a radio tower. The glass tower at the top once carried the station's call letters.

When it opened, the building had an F.W. Woolworth retail store on its ground floor. WCAU had eight studios—including one that could fit the entire Philadelphia Orchestra—and a signal so strong the station could be picked up by most of the eastern United States.

Another Art Deco gem, Suburban Station, is only few blocks north at 16th Street and JFK Boulevard. The block-long building constructed in 1930 houses offices, retail shops, and a major commuter rail station.

The former WCAU building remains one of the most striking examples of Art Deco architecture in the city. (Photo by Tricia Pompilio.)

In 1952, WCAU moved to a larger building that had both radio and television studios as TV became America's preferred medium. The Art Institute of Philadelphia took over the property in the 1980s, giving it a complete rehab that included studding the facade with broken blue glass. Its current owners rent the space for retail and offices.

THIS USED TO BE: WCAU Radio Headquarters

NOW IT'S: Retail and office space

LOCATION: Center City

Built to Dazzle

When it opened on Christmas Day 1928, the Boyd Theatre was a true movie palace, an Art Deco–style masterpiece with an ornate, welcoming ticket booth and an auditorium that could seat almost 2,500 people while accommodating a full orchestra. Its multi-floor lobby, one of the few design elements that remains, was built to dazzle, lined with mirrors and mosaics.

But for Philadelphians in the late 1920s, one of the most overwhelming elements was the screen and what was played upon it. The *Philadelphia Inquirer* made special note of the opening night "featuring Paramount's first all-talking picture, *Interference*." A post-screening review complained that "it is a picture with many words and no music. It might as well be the stage play," and that the new theater was a bit too fancy "with all of its multiple comforts, presented in the bizarre notes of extreme modernism, is a sight that will always hold something new for the love of the 'different.'"

The Boyd hosted exclusive first runs of classics, including *The Wizard of Oz* (1939) and *Gone with the Wind* (1940). In 1949, Philadelphia-born singer Mario Lanza was in attendance for the world premiere of his first movie, *That Midnight Kiss*. In 1952, Philadelphia's Princess, Grace Kelly, attended the opening of her film *High Noon*. In 1993, actors Tom Hanks and Denzel Washington were here for the world premiere of their Academy Award–winning film *Philadelphia*.

In 2002, United Artists sold the theater to developers. The property bounced between owners for a few years before one received city approval to build a 24-story apartment tower rising from where the former auditorium had been. Only the Boyd's facade and parts of its ornate lobby remain.

In the 1920s and '30s, Aldine Theater, which was also on this block, refused to seat African Americans. That sparked public protests and is thought to have aided the passage of Pennsylvania's 1935 Equal Rights Law.

The exterior of the Boyd Theatre hints at the former magnificence of its interior. (Photo by Tricia Pompilio.)

The Sameric Corporation purchased the theater in 1971 and renamed it. (Image courtesy of the Free Library of Philadelphia.)

THIS USED TO BE: Boyd Theatre

NOW IT'S: Harper Apartments

LOCATION: Center City

This Business Sold Everything from Plastic Spoons to Hot Dog Carts

Louis Eidelson got his start in the housewares business as a door-to-door salesman, peddling cups, saucers, pots, and pans from a horse and wagon in New York. In 1927, he and his wife, Bella, opened Trenton China Pottery, a mom-and-pop restaurant supply company offering new and used products. It was the first business of its kind in Philadelphia. Its "ghost sign" is the only remaining clue that the business was here.

The Eidelsons named their business after the New Jersey capital because that's where they purchased their merchandise. Their son told the *Philadelphia Daily News* in 2000 that his father was a Russian immigrant. "His English was not too good, but his math was . . . Dad would drive there in a Model T and bring back a load of plates, cups, saucers." The company sold more than 50,000 products, ranging from single spoons to hot dog vending carts.

That small one-store business eventually grew to encompass 55,000 square feet and nine separate buildings. The property was sold to private developers in 2011 but the buildings have sat empty since then. Trenton China Pottery, now T.C.P. Restaurant Equipment Co., moved its operations to the city's Port Richmond neighborhood. It is still family-owned.

The Fireman's Hall Museum, 147 North 2nd Street, is located about a block away. Its exhibits detail the history of firefighting over the last 300 years.

Trenton China Pottery was the city's first restaurant supply company. Its buildings, and its ghost signage, remain today. (Photo by Tricia Pompilio.)

THIS USED TO BE: Trenton China Pottery

NOW IT'S: Empty Buildings

LOCATION: Old City

First Baptist Church of Philadelphia Cemetery (page 44)
(Photo by Tricia Pompilio.)

Philadelphia Savings Fund Society (page 32)
(Photo by Tricia Pompilio.)

Keebler-Weyl Baking Company (page 58)
(Photo by Tricia Pompilio.)

Municipal Pier 11 (page 190)
(Photo by Tricia Pompilio.)

N.W. Ayer & Son Advertising (page 48)
(Photo by Tricia Pompilio.)

Boyd Theatre (page 84)
(Photo by Tricia Pompilio.)

Satterlee Hospital (page 6)
(Photo by Tricia Pompilio.)

Merchants' Exchange (page 50)
(Photo by Tricia Pompilio.)

Farm Journal Building (page 46)
(Photo by Tricia Pompilio.)

Rebecca Gratz Club (page 36)
(Photo by Tricia Pompilio.)

ON THIS SIT
SLATE RO
WILLIAM PEN
AND PENNSYLV
MENT

Slate Roof House (page 10)
(Photo by Tricia Pompilio.)

Burk Brothers Tannery and Leather Factory (page 20)
(Photo by Tricia Pompilio.)

National Products Co. (page 107)
(Photo by Tricia Pompilio.)

Oliver H. Bair Funeral Home (page 79)
(Photo by Tricia Pompilio.)

A Facade to Remember

In 1929, 17-year-old Harry Caplen opened National Products Co., a housewares store, in Old City. He used the $600 he'd earned selling chewing gum on the ferry docks to pay his rent and buy his starter inventory.

Caplen's business would grow to become one of the country's largest restaurant suppliers, commanding 20,000 square feet of space that included four warehouses and a five-story showroom. He unified this block-and-a-half complex by building an orange-tiled facade that he hoped was "bold enough to draw customers away from the area's competing restaurant suppliers," his son Neil told the *Philadelphia Inquirer* in 2015. "He turned it into a landmark."

Caplen was an old-fashioned businessman, sealing deals with handshakes and offering customers loans without filing any paperwork. He stressed customer service, telling the *Philadelphia Daily News* in 1990, "No order is too small. I'll break up a box of supplies to sell a single $7 unit to a restaurateur and I'll deliver it, too, because I know that customer is likely to order $7,000 worth of supplies the next time."

National Products Co. closed in 1996. When developers purchased the property in 2012, they promised to recreate the facade to front this residential development that includes a 10-story high-rise, two six-story mid-rise buildings, and 26 townhomes.

The National is less than a block from Elfreth's Alley, which is located between North 2nd and North Front Streets It is the oldest continuously occupied street in the United States, with 32 houses built between 1703 and 1836.

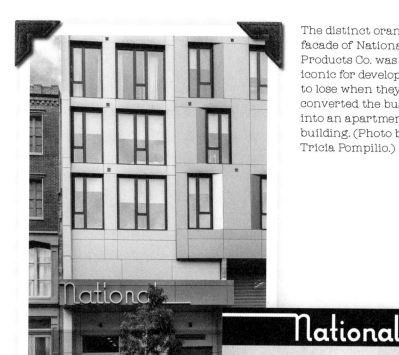

The distinct orange facade of National Products Co. was too iconic for developers to lose when they converted the business into an apartment building. (Photo by Tricia Pompilio.)

Renters began moving into the newly restored National in 2018. (Image courtesy of Todd Kimmel/The Grand Review Studio).

THIS USED TO BE: National Products Co.

NOW IT'S: The National - Apartments

LOCATION: Old City

Bananas, Root Beer, and a Beaux Arts Beauty

The 1876 World's Fair, the first to be held in the United States, drew 10 million people from across the world to Fairmount Park. The first building completed as part of the Centennial Exhibition was Memorial Hall, which now houses the Please Touch Children's Museum.

About 200 buildings were specially constructed for the exposition, but Memorial Hall was the only one that drew the attention of President Ulysses S. Grant, who attended its dedication. It was built to be fireproof, made of granite, marble, and ornamental plaster; only the doors were wood. The Beaux Arts architecture includes a dome topped with a 23-foot-tall statue of Columbia, the female personification of the United States, holding a laurel branch.

The Fair ran from May 10 to November 10, drawing visitors from 37 countries. The exhibition showcased American ingenuity: Thomas Edison displayed his automatic telegraph system. George Westinghouse and George Eastman also exhibited their new inventions.

Alexander Graham Bell was the talk of the Fair. He publicly demonstrated what his newly patented telephone could do with two of his devices 20 feet apart. Bell used one to call the other, which was answered by Brazil's Emperor Pedro. Hearing Bell's voice through the receiver, Pedro exclaimed, "It speaks!"

The Fair introduced the country to bananas, which were eaten with a knife and fork; Hires Root Beer; and Heinz Tomato Ketchup. Visitors

Ohio House, nearby at 4700 States Drive, is the park's only other surviving World's Fair structure. It was built from sandstones, each carved with the name of the Ohio quarry where it originated.

Memorial Hall houses one of the country's best children's museums. (Public Domain, wikipedia.org.)

Memorial Hall is one of the few surviving buildings from the 1876 World's Fair in Philadelphia. (Detroit Publishing Co., Memorial Hall, Fairmount Park, Philadelphia. Photograph. Retrieved from the Library of Congress, www.loc.gov/item/2016800221/.)

gawked at the hand and torch of the Statue of Liberty as the rest of her body was being engineered in France.

In 2008, Please Touch Museum, a museum for children seven and younger, opened to visitors in what was once Memorial Hall.

THIS USED TO BE: Memorial Hall

NOW IT'S: Please Touch Museum

LOCATION: Fairmount Park

A Savvy Dairy Known for Its Ads as Well as Its Products

Give Abbott Alderney Dairy some credit: When it came to advertising, the company wasn't messing around.

The company played on parental guilt, promising that its farmers were "trained in the art of producing pure milk ... Surely your child is entitled to this kind of milk." It promoted its cutting-edge technology, boasting that its ice cream was sold "*in a sanitary paraffined carton*, into which Abbotts Ice Cream, *is filled direct from the freezer, untouched by hands.*" (Emphasis theirs.) It appealed to women's vanity. One 1968 newspaper ad featured a sketch of a woman standing on a scale and smiling. "Today is Wednesday. By Saturday, you can lose up to 5 lbs. with Abbotts amazing Cottage Cheese diet. Free diet with carton."

And it got the kids on board, giving away free ice cream and publishing the 1926 book *Raggedy Ann and Maizie Moocow*. In the story, Mister Meenie has stolen Maizie's ice cream freezer. Raggedy Ann and Andy help Maizie get it back, then they "enjoy an ice cream party, demonstrating the healthy (and tasty) benefits of dairy products."

Farmer George Abbott founded the dairy in Salem, New Jersey, in 1876. It grew quickly, expanding into Philadelphia at the turn of the twentieth century, and then moved into the Midwest.

The company built this structure in 1921, using it for offices and a retail store. Alderney is a breed of cow from the British Channel Islands known for producing rich milk. The pure breed line is now extinct, although there are still hybrids available.

If reading about sweet treats has left you craving one, check out D'Emilio's Old World Ice Treats, which is about five blocks away at 1928 East Passyunk Avenue.

Abbott Alderney Dairy was founded in neighboring New Jersey in 1876. This facility closed in 1964. (Photo by Tricia Pompilio.)

THIS USED TO BE: Abbott Alderney Dairy

NOW IT'S: Residence and business space

LOCATION: Point Breeze/Newbold

When Things Are Poppin' the Philadelphia Way

For almost 40 years, one television show set the musical tone for most of the United States: *American Bandstand*, which debuted to Philadelphia audiences in 1952.

The earliest incarnation of the show—simply called *Bandstand*—was filmed in Philadelphia's WFIL-TV's Studio B. Teens between 14 and 18 spent up to three hours lined up outside hoping for a spot on the dance floor. As one participant later described the process to *Parade* magazine, "Hundreds were turned away. So getting through the red doors and being on the show meant you were part of a small, special, elite group. Walking into Studio B was like stepping out of Kansas and into Oz."

Rock music was still new when the show debuted and many from the older generation regarded it with suspicion. Clean-cut Dick Clark, who brought the rebranded *American Bandstand* to national audiences in 1957, was there to assuage their fears. The show required males to wear a jacket and tie or sweater. Girls wore dresses or skirts—but not anything too tight. One of the producers theorized that "when you dressed right, you behaved right."

Each show would feature lip-synched performances by up-and-coming artists. *Bandstand* was the American television debut for performers like Neil Diamond, The Jackson 5, Sonny and Cher, Bon Jovi, and the Norwegian band *a-ha*. The show became known for launching national dance crazes; the first was Chubby Checker's The Twist in 1960. Others included The Stroll, Mashed Potato, The Jerk, and The Hustle.

The Enterprise Center had a display of *American Bandstand* memorabilia in what was once Studio B, which is now used as a conference room.

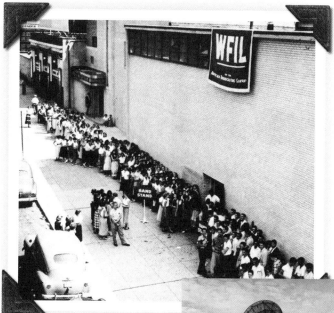

Teenagers were willing to stand in line for three hours for an opportunity to dance on the afternoon music show. (Photo courtesy of the Free Library of Philadelphia.)

The Enterprise Center purchased the building in 1995. Because of its historic significance, an endowment fund covers ongoing maintenance. (Photo by Tricia Pompilio.)

Another popular segment was "Rate-A-Record," during which two of the teen dancers would rate a new song. The kids weren't music critics and their reviews were almost always basic: "It's got a good beat and you can dance to it."

In 1964, the show moved to California.

THIS USED TO BE: American Bandstand Studio

NOW IT'S: The Enterprise Center

LOCATION: West Philadelphia

Before Hollywood There Was Betzwood

Before Metro-Goldwyn-Mayer, before Cecil B. DeMille, even before Hollywood . . . there was Siegmund Lubin and Betzwood.

Lubin was one of America's first movie moguls. Born in Prussia, Lubin emigrated to the United States as a young man, settling in Philadelphia around 1883. An optician by trade, he became interested in creating moving pictures after seeing an early model of a movie projector.

In 1896, he made his first film—of his horse eating hay. A year later, he developed and offered for sale his own camera and projectors, prompting Thomas Edison to sue him for copyright infringement and launching a legal battle that dragged on for years.

Lubin began making silent films on the rooftop of a building at 912 Arch Street, staging everything from Biblical stories to so-called gentlemen's smokers featuring local women doing risqué things, like bathing. (The building was in the heart of the city's red-light district.) His studio's logo was the Liberty Bell and his brand message the words "Clear as a Bell," which referred to the sharpness of the images and not the sound quality.

A Lubinville film in the works. (Image courtesy of the Free Library of Philadelphia.)

To meet the public's ravenous demand for films, Lubin began building cinemas along the East Coast while also ramping up film production. In 1910, he built a state-of-the-art studio—dubbed Lubinville—in North Philadelphia. Made almost entirely of glass and steel, the building had four stages and employed

The legal fighting between Lubin and Edison lasted about a decade, ending in 1908 when Lubin and other producers joined Edison in founding the Motion Picture Patents Company.

Siegmund Lubin's open-air silent film studio on Arch Street in 1899. (Public domain, wikipedia.com.)

Lubin also owned movie theaters, including the Lubin Nickelodeon on Chestnut Street, seen here in 1907. (Image courtesy of the Library Company of Philadelphia.)

hundreds of people. He also purchased the 350-acre Betzwood estate in a rural area outside Philadelphia. The two locations combined employed more than 500 people.

Lubin's company produced more than 3,000 silent films before financial mismanagement and a devastating fire forced him to file for bankruptcy. While his name is not widely known today, Lubin had the respect of his peers. After his death in 1932 at age 82, a group that included Charlie Chaplin, Douglas Fairbanks, and the Mayer and Goldwyn of MGM donated money to his struggling widow.

THIS USED TO BE: Lubin Studios

NOW IT'S: Parking garage

LOCATION: Center City

No Drinking or Gambling, but the Food Was Cheap

The building that would become the Divine Lorraine was completed in 1894, but its story begins in 1948. That's when Reverend Major Jealous Divine, a spiritual leader whose thousands of followers believed he was God, purchased the building at the corner of North Broad Street and Fairmount Avenue as a home for his faithful.

Father Divine, as he was best known, founded the International Peace Mission Movement in New York at the start of the Great Depression. He preached racial equality, promoted celibacy even in marriage, and believed in economic independence, eschewing credit. Critics called Divine a cult leader.

Divine's followers often turned over their savings when they joined his movement. Divine helped them find jobs and monitored their earnings thereafter. Before its leader's death in 1965, the movement had a property portfolio worth about $10 million and included hotels, farms, and Woodmont, a 73-acre estate in the Philadelphia suburb of Gladwyne that is still owned and operated by the Peace Mission Movement.

Father Divine paid $485,000 cash for the 10-story building, the equivalent of almost $5 million in today's dollars. Residents—and any guests—were expected to follow certain rules: smoking, drinking, drug use, gambling, and the use of profanity were forbidden. Women were required to wear skirts and not allowed makeup or perfume. Men and women lived on separate floors. Even married couples were expected to stay apart when visiting.

Father Divine's former home in nearby Gladwyn, Woodmont Estate, is still owned and operated by his Peace Mission Movement. It is open to the public, containing Divine's library and a museum.

The Divine Lorraine remains one of the city's most beloved buildings. (Photo by Tricia Pompilio.)

Some parts of Divine's building were open to the public, including a 10th floor worship area and the first-floor kitchen which offered daily lunches for twenty-five cents. Guests were encouraged to take all that they could eat, but to eat all that they took.

The Peace Mission moved out of the Divine Lorraine in 1999. After a $44 million renovation, the building reopened as an apartment complex in 2018.

THIS USED TO BE: The Divine Lorraine Hotel– International Peace Mission Movement Residences and Headquarters

NOW IT'S: The Divine Lorraine Hotel – Apartments with restaurants and retail space

LOCATION: Fairmount

"If One Was Incurable, Insane, Consumptive, Blind, Orphaned, Crippled, Destitute or Senile..."

In the mid-1800s, Philadelphia officials moved the overcrowded Philadelphia Almshouse, which provided government care to the poor, from its downtown location to what they considered the hinterlands, across the Schuylkill River. The purpose, as author Robert Morris Skaler wrote in a history of the neighborhood, was "to remove the pauper class, the insane, the sickly from Center City.... By the end of the 19th century, if one was incurable, insane, consumptive, blind, orphaned, crippled, destitute or senile, one would most likely end up in a faith-based charitable institution or asylum in West Philadelphia."

The facility, known to locals as Old Blockley or Blockley Hospital, fell under the care umbrella of Philadelphia General Hospital, which had been established in the 1700s. The transition had inauspicious beginnings. One of the first major newspaper accounts of events there came in July 1864, when the roof of the three-story building housing the Department of Insane Females collapsed. As the *Philadelphia Inquirer* reported, "At least eighteen poor imbeciles, all females, with the exception of an idiotic and deformed boy, six years of age, were instantly killed..."

Change came slowly. In the 1880s, Alice Fisher, who had studied at London's Florence Nightingale Training School, reorganized the facility's nursing program, launching a rigorous training regimen that made the

Philadelphia has been a hub of American medicine since its very beginnings. Even today one out of every six doctors in the United States is trained in the city.

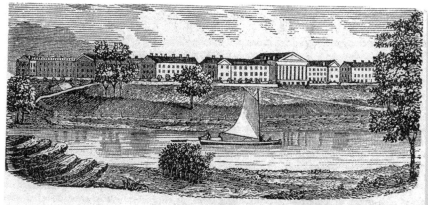

Blockley Almshouse.

City leaders moved the almshouse away from Center City across the Schuylkill River to West Philadelphia. (Images courtesy of the Free Library of Philadelphia.)

PHILADELPHIA HOSPITAL AND BLOCKLEY ALMSHOUSE, 34th and Pine

term "Blockley Nurse" an honor as it described highly trained, committed caregivers distinguished by their double-frill cap.

In the 1910s, government leaders and private citizens raised funds to further improve the facility. PGH, as it was called, added buildings and beds and recruited prominent physicians. When it closed in 1977, the institution was respected not only for its high standards but also for its commitment to care for all regardless of insurance or income.

THIS USED TO BE: Old Blockley

NOW IT'S: Children's Hospital of Philadelphia

LOCATION: West Philadelphia

She Was Serena Williams before Serena Williams Was Born

Ora Washington's name is little known today, but she was one of the most talented American female athletes of the first half of the twentieth century. Her legacy is largely overlooked or unknown because she was African American.

Washington honed her skills at this branch of the Germantown YWCA. In 1917, the building was set aside for the exclusive use of African American women and girls. It was also a hub of civil rights activity. Its committee on race relations sponsored events including an art exhibition featuring the works of African American artists, interracial tea parties, and "Negro Achievement Week."

Washington excelled on both the tennis and basketball courts. One year after she'd picked up a racket, she won a national championship in a tournament for Black players. In the years that followed, she won multiple tournaments, sometimes going years without a loss, and held the American Tennis Association's national title from 1929 to 1936.

Washington was also a basketball star, playing center for the *Philadelphia Tribune*'s basketball team. The team was so good it lost only a handful of games in the 1930s.

In a 1988 *New York Times* essay, tennis great Arthur Ashe wrote that Washington "may have been the best female athlete ever." *Philadelphia Inquirer* columnist Frank Fitzpatrick described Washington as "Serena

The YWCA's main Germantown branch was located nearby at 5820-24 Germantown Avenue. It, too, is now closed. *Philadelphia Inquirer* architecture critic Inga Saffron wrote in 2015, "Without the YWCA, Germantown wouldn't be Germantown."

The Germantown YWCA was integral to the growth of the neighborhood and where Ora Washington learned how to play basketball and tennis. (Image courtesy of the Preservation Alliance of Greater Philadelphia.)

Ora Washington with just a few of her championship trophies. (Image courtesy of *Philadelphia Tribune*/ John W. Mosley Photograph Collection, Charles L. Blockson Afro-American Collection, Temple University Libraries.)

Williams before Serena Williams, winning virtually all the tennis tournaments—and winning them numerous times."

Washington's athletic prowess prompted President Franklin D. Roosevelt's administration to build public tennis courts in heavily African American neighborhoods. Ashe and Althea Gibson, the first African American male and female to win Wimbledon and the US Open, learned the game as children on these courts.

Before her death in 1971, Washington coached multiple sports at the YWCA where her athletic career began.

THIS USED TO BE: Germantown YWCA

NOW IT'S: Empty Building

LOCATION: Germantown

The Mother of the LGBTQ Rights Movement

Barbara Gittings is often called the mother of the LGBTQ movement, publicly fighting for equal rights when homosexuality was considered a mental illness and, in some places, a crime. She and Frank Kameny, credited as the father of the LGBTQ movement, helped organize the earliest public gay rights demonstrations in Philadelphia, New York, and Washington, DC, years before the Stonewall Inn uprising in 1969.

Gittings was 18 when she left her family home in Wilmington, DE, her departure prompted by her father's anger when he found a lesbian romance novel in her bedroom. He told her to burn the book, a message he communicated by note as he did not want to speak to her.

Gittings and Kameny spent years protesting the American Psychiatric Association's classification of homosexuality as a mental disorder that could be treated with electric shock therapy or lobotomy. The organization finally removed homosexuality from that list in 1973, prompting Kameny to quip that in a single day "we were cured en masse."

While not trained as a librarian, Gittings worked with the American Library Association's Gay Task Force to catalogue and expand collections

Check out the mural *Pride and Progress* painted on one side of the William Way Community Center, 1315 Spruce Street. It celebrates Philadelphia's role in the fight for LGBTQ equality. Gittings is depicted on the left side wearing a rainbow shirt. Also, the stretch of Locust Street between South 12th and 13th Streets is called Barbara Gittings Way.

(Photo by Tricia Pompilio.)

Barbara Gittings is often called the mother of the LGBTQ movement. (Public domain, wikipedia.org.)

of LGBTQ literature. Gittings said she did so after struggling to find appropriate literature when she was trying to understand her blooming sexuality, often finding relevant information under headings including "sexual perversion" and "sexual aberration."

Gittings died in 2007. The Free Library of Philadelphia's LGBTQ collection is named in her honor.

THIS USED TO BE: Home of Barbara Gittings

NOW IT'S: Locust Commons, an apartment building

LOCATION: Center City

From Trikes to Trig

In the early 1900s, the A. Mecky Company was one of the city's most successful manufacturers of "juvenile wheeled goods," which included baby carriages, tricycles, wagons, wheelbarrows, scooters, and the Velo-King Velocipede Tricycles, its most popular product. It built its headquarters here around 1913.

German immigrant August Mecky founded his company in 1883 after seeing a hole in the "mechanical horse" market. Children were more likely to ride wheeled vehicles propelled by pedal, but advertising and manufacturing instead focused on machines for adults. Mecky was the first to market directly to children, usually focusing on boys, but also running a 1928 ad that began "Girls – The 'VeloKing' Bike Is Now Here," later noting the machine's "beauty, swiftness and easy riding."

As a backup, the company addressed ads to parents: "Here's health and pleasure and outdoor fun for your kiddie!" and "We know something about the average Dad's and Mother's desire for their children to have the best and safest!"

When Mecky died in 1909, his *Philadelphia Inquirer* obituary described him as a "well-known manufacturer of children's coaches and vehicles." Mecky's son-in-law Richard Ledig took over the company's management, designing and getting patents on products, including a bicycle that could be converted to a scooter, a child-sized car operated by foot power that had "almost everything but the oil tank," and walking pull toys that could "run, walk and waddle." He also manufactured small appliances, creating the "Twin Bowl, Triple Purpose" toaster, the "aristocrat of the breakfast table" that could toast bread, boil eggs without water, and cook sausages at the same time.

Cristo Rey serves students with limited financial resources. Every student works five days per month at a Philadelphia business. The school says that 100 percent of its graduates attend four-year colleges.

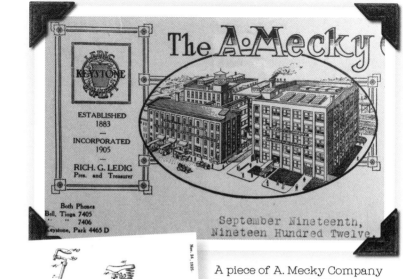

A piece of A. Mecky Company letterhead circa 1920. Note the reference to "Ledig Keystone Quality." LeDig is Richard Ledig, the son-in-law who took over the company after founder August Mecky's death. Pennsylvania is known as "the Keystone State" because of the key position it held geographically, politically and economically in the nation's founding. (Public domain.)

The company was an innovator in the field. (Image courtesy of the Pennsylvania State Historical Preservation Office.)

The original A. Mecky building sat empty for decades before Cristo Rey Philadelphia High School purchased the property in 2017 and spent $40 million to incorporate it as part of a new seven-acre campus.

THIS USED TO BE: A. Mecky Bike Factory

NOW IT'S: Cristo Rey Philadelphia High School

LOCATION: Nicetown/Tioga

Of Soap and Suitcases

At two different times in the twentieth century, the 12-story building at North 22nd and Arch Streets housed a multimillion-dollar business that was a game-changer in its industry: the Larkin Soap Company and the Belber Trunk and Bag Company.

The New York–based Larkin Soap Company built this high-rise in 1900. The company knew how to market: It was the first to include small "thank you" trinkets in its packages, like the "fine Japanese silk scarf" that came with its Elite toilet soap and the white towel that accompanied its Ocean Bath body soap.

The company recruited housewives—called "Larkin Secretaries"—and encouraged them to sell products door-to-door. The Larkin Secretaries—there were more than 90,000 at one time—established 10-member "Larkin Clubs." Each club member promised to purchase $1 of Larkin products per month, then shared the premiums—like housewares or rebates—that the company provided.

The company also promoted "the Larkin Idea," a mail-order business that in 1920 employed 2,000 people and had sales of more than $28 million, the equivalent of $365 million today.

The Belber Trunk and Bag Company purchased the Larkin building in 1920 as its main office, factory, and salesroom. Its motto was "As Modern as Tomorrow." Its innovations included making bags and trunks out of lighter materials, developing new locking mechanisms, and offering a steamer trunk curtain that held clothes firmly in place. The company was the first to sell luggage as sets.

Hollywood actors carried Belber luggage in travel-related movies. Its print ads boasted of its attractive look: "Luxury luggage at a far from luxury price" and durability: "Before you buy luggage, consider the fraternity of baggage smashers that's going to handle it."

The building became loft condominiums in 2006.

The building is near Schuylkill River Park, 300 South 25th Street, which offers running trails, a playground, and tennis courts.

SEPTEMBER NUMBER 1902

The Larkin Idea

MEET ME AT THE LARKIN EXHIBIT
SOAPS—PREMIUMS
AT THE
MECHANICS FAIR, BOSTON.
MECHANICS BUILDING,
HUNTINGTON AVE.,
Sept. 22, to Nov.1, 1902.

The building at 2200 Arch Street was reborn as condominiums in 2006. It has 165 units. (Photo by Tricia Pompilio.)

The Larkin Soap Company was a mail-order pioneer. (Public domain, wikipedia.org.)

THIS USED TO BE: Larkin Soap Co./Belber Trunk and Bag Co.

NOW IT'S: 2200 Arch Street Loft Condominiums

LOCATION: Spring Garden

The Opossum of Protection, the Squirrel of Frugality

With business booming at the turn of the century, the Fidelity Mutual Life Insurance Company commissioned this massive Art Deco structure on a two-acre lot as its headquarters in 1928. The dramatic arched main entrance is believed to be the most elaborate of its kind made in the twentieth century.

The words engraved above the main entrance on Pennsylvania Avenue are: "In the honor and perpetuity of the family is founded the state. In the nobler life of the household is the nobler life of mankind." The 26th Street side carries this message: "He labors best who loves best: the finest work of a man's life is to open the doors of opportunity to those who depend on him."

Sculptor Lee Lawrie, one of the most celebrated architectural sculptors of his time, created dozens of Egyptian-inspired reliefs that adorn the building, including those of the five animals that represent the attributes of insurance: the opossum of protection, the owl of wisdom, the dog of fidelity, the pelican of charity, and the squirrel of frugality. For reasons unknown, the squirrels are most prominently on display.

Fidelity Mutual Life occupied the building until 1972. The Philadelphia Museum of Art took over in 1999 and renamed it the Ruth and Raymond G. Perelman Building to honor longtime museum supporters. It houses six galleries totaling 2,000 square feet of exhibition space, a library, the museum's costumes and textiles collection, and more than 150,000 modern and contemporary prints, drawings, and photographs.

Tickets for admission to the building are included in the price of a Philadelphia Museum of Art ticket or can be purchased separately.

The "squirrel of frugality" sits on the top corners of the Perelman Building. (Photo by Tricia Pompilio.)

A close-up of the frugal squirrel sculpture. (Photo courtesy of Waymarking.)

THIS USED TO BE: Fidelity Mutual Life Insurance Company

NOW IT'S: Philadelphia Museum of Art's Ruth and Raymond G. Perelman Building

LOCATION: Fairmount

Homeopathy Comes to America

More than a century before the construction of the Pennsylvania Convention Center in the 1990s, two properties integral to the city's development stood near the intersection of North 12th and Race Streets: the home of Constantine Hering, cofounder of Hahnemann Hospital, and—later—the printing factory owned by his son, Walter. These businesses helped establish Philadelphia as a leader in the fields of medicine and publishing.

In the early 1800s, German medical student Constantine Hering injured a finger and developed gangrene. Doctors recommended amputation. Instead, Hering successfully treated himself using methods pioneered by Samuel Hahnemann, the father of homeopathic medicine. The incident changed Hering's life. As he later wrote, "To Hahnemann, who had saved my finger, I gave my whole hand, and to the promulgation of his teaching, not only my hand, but the entire man, body and soul." He and two colleagues founded Philadelphia's Hahnemann Medical College and Hospital in 1848.

The doctor's son Walter was 12 years old in 1868 when he purchased a five-dollar printing press and began selling business cards and prescription pads to his father's colleagues. The elder Hering built his son a small printing press on land next to the family home. The business grew quickly, eventually specializing in tickets. Walter Hering's Globe Ticket Company became a leader in its industry. It remains one of the country's largest today.

In 1900, Walter Hering built an eight-story factory on the land where his father's house and original print shop once stood. The building's front bore a bas relief of Dr. Hering's head and a Latin inscription that translated to "Constantine Hering lived here and this is where he died July 23, 1880."

The Pennsylvania Convention Center has about one million square feet of exhibit space.

Globe Ticket remains an industry leader. It is now headquartered in Illinois. (Photo courtesy of Globe Ticket.)

Constantine Hering is sometimes called the father of American homeopathy. (Public domain, wikipedia.org.)

Cheap Shoes Did Not Interest Him

Until its nearly century-long run ended in 1965, Laird, Schober & Company was known for such high quality shoes that one newspaper reported that a group of visiting French shoemakers declared, "Magnifique!" after examining the company's goods. For more than 20 years, its fine footwear was made here.

The company was founded in 1870 by a partnership that included brothers Samuel and John Laird and their brother-in-law, George Schober. From the start, the emphasis was on quality. The company's ads boasted its use of the finest materials: imported patent leather, silk tassels, linen, and calf leather. A 1934 article in *Binghamton* (NY) *Press and Sun-Bulletin* said this about George Laird, the shoe company's second-generation leader: "His business maxim is as concise and simple as this: 'I made it a point not to compete in low price but always to compete in the high quality of goods which I made.' Cheap shoes do not interest Mr. Laird any more than imitation diamonds interest Tiffany."

A 1915 ad in the *Delaware County Daily Times* promoted "New Welted Pumps, with vamps and heels of patent colt and quarters of white calf" on sale for five dollars, equal to about $129 today.

For half the cost of a pair of Laird Schober shoes circa 1915, one could get the following at Trader Joe's today: six Apple Cider Donuts, a pound of Toscano cheese, a 12-ounce bag of whole bean coffee from Nicaragua, a 16-ounce package of *Spaghetti Cacio e Pepe*, two pounds of Harissa-flavored chicken thighs, a pesto pasta veggie sauté kit, corn tortilla chips, a bottle of Platinum Reserve Cabernet Yountville, and organic garlic naan crackers. (Total: $62.92, before applicable taxes)

A testament to Laird Shober's quality? Its shoes are sold today on ebay. (Public domain.)

Two fashion businesses once called this building home: shoemaker Laird, Schober & Company and the After Six formalwear company. (Photo by Tricia Pompilio.)

The company invested in cutting-edge manufacturing equipment, including one machine that could sew soles on 100 pairs of shoes in one hour and another that could create 100,000 button holes per week. Its corporate culture was such that some employees spent their entire careers on the job. The 1934 article noted that of its 1,000 plant employees, 250 of them " ... have been with the firm 25 years or more. One cutter has been 61 years, one shoemaker 59 years, others 55 and 52 years with the firm."

The shoemaker moved into a new facility in the late 1940s. The building's next occupant was After Six, the formalwear company, which used it as its corporate offices and main manufacturing plant until 1985.

THIS USED TO BE: Laird, Schober & Company

NOW IT'S: Trader Joe's Grocery Store and Apartments

LOCATION: Center City West

Where All People Were Welcome

Greenbelt Knoll was the city's first planned, racially integrated neighborhood, a collection of 19 homes built on three sides of Pennypack Park in 1956. Developer Morris Milgram had married into a real estate family but balked at building homes "that all people couldn't live in," he told *United Press International* in 1960. He aimed to create communities with a roughly even number of white and minority residents.

Until his death at age 81 in 1997, Milgram "provided integrated housing for 20,000 people in 15 states.... A dreamer and a doer, Mr. Milgram was always ready to challenge authority and accepted ways," his *Philadelphia Inquirer* obituary noted.

Milgram was part of the first wave of Greenbelt Knoll residents, joining the families of Robert N.C. Nix Sr., the first African American to represent Pennsylvania in Congress; Pulitzer Prize–winning playwright Charles Fuller; and Rev. Leon Sullivan, whose anti-apartheid efforts changed South Africa.

In a 1957 letter to the *Inquirer*, Greenbelt Knoll residents urged other communities to welcome integration instead of protesting it as if the area had "not progressed beyond the 19th century or the Civil War."

"We believe that division and strife, weakening the American tradition, result in a large measure, because we and our children, restricted by these 'all-white' and 'all-Black' patterns of community living, have not had an opportunity to know each other," it read in part. "Negro and non-Negro families, have found friendship, understanding, and much satisfaction in the way in which the community is developing."

Pennypack Park is 1,600 acres of woodlands, rolling hills, and open meadows along the Pennypack Creek with miles of paved and unpaved trails for hiking, biking, running, and horseback riding.

a community with a contemporary concept . . .

Contemporary is more than a word at Greenbelt Knoll . . . it is a way of life . . . casual, relaxed living that gives you a new sense of freedom and contentment.

Greenbelt Knoll is a community of only nineteen homes (of which 16 have already been sold at the time of printing) set in a tract of towering oaks and tulip poplars, surrounded by 1200 acres of quiet woodland. Although Greenbelt Knoll is within city limits, with all city services, its country atmosphere is unaffected by the tensions of the city. Here at Greenbelt Knoll the creative mind is stimulated to continual advancement.

Greenbelt Knoll homes are designed with a dramatic new architectural concept that has received the acclaim of the foremost authorities in home planning.

The architecture blends so harmoniously with the woodland surroundings that the homes seem to grow from the very earth on which they stand.

Greenbelt Knoll is a friendly, democratic community of congenial families including engineers, educators, doctors, psychiatrists, social workers, industrial designer, attorney, a fire department officer, insurance executive, accountant, minister, and a builder, Morris Milgram, executive vice president of Greenbelt Knoll, Inc.

These truly contemporary homes have a 27 foot living room with a triangular brick fireplace set in a floor-to-ceiling glass wall, 3 to 5 bedrooms, 1½ to 2½ baths, large patio, huge beamed overhangs that extend from the exterior into the living room. Exteriors are of redwood, mahogany or cypress with matching paneling in the living room. The homes are set so that no two living areas face each other, affording utmost privacy. Greenbelt Knoll homes are priced from $22,500.

food fashions family furnishings   THE NEW YORK TIMES, FRIDAY SEPTEMBER 5, 1969

A Microcosm of Integrated Life

This sales brochure from Greenbelt Knoll sells it as an urban enclave. (Image courtesy of Pennsylvania Historical Society.)

(Greenbelt Knoll, featured in *The New York Times*, Sept. 5, 1969, via placesjournal.org.)

THIS USED TO BE: Greenbelt Knoll

NOW IT'S: Residential Neighborhood

LOCATION: Holmesburg

"Observing, Drawing and Painting the People of America"

Artist Dox Thrash's depictions of African Americans in the first half of the twentieth century highlighted the many similarities—and notable differences—between their experiences and those of white Americans. As he wrote in his memoirs, he spent his career "observing, drawing and painting the people of America, especially the Negro."

Born in Georgia in 1893, Thrash always knew he wanted to be an artist. As a teenager, he moved north as part of the Great Migration, working as an elevator operator to pay for classes at the Art Institute of Chicago. His education was interrupted by World War I when he joined the Army's African American regiment known as the Buffalo Soldiers. He was soon on the front lines in Europe and was seriously injured the day before the 1918 Armistice was signed.

Thrash returned to Chicago after a long stay in a French military hospital, finishing his art education with the help of federal funding. He moved to Philadelphia in 1926, painting signs, designing corporate logos, and creating promotional posters while working on his own artistic pursuits. Before his death in 1965, Thrash had exhibitions at esteemed institutions including the Smithsonian Institute, Howard University, the Library of Congress, and the Philadelphia Museum of Art.

When Thrash lived in this corner home, the neighborhood was a hub for artists and musicians. John Coltrane and Duke Ellington performed at nearby concert venues. The Pyramid Club, the African American social club nearby, hosted speakers including Martin Luther King Jr.

The Philadelphia Museum of Art, 2600 Benjamin Franklin Parkway, has multiple Thrash works in its collections. He also has work in the Baltimore Museum of Art's permanent collection.

Detail of the etching "Twenty-Fourth Street and Ridge Avenue" by Dox Thrash. (Image courtesy of FEDERAL WORKS AGENCY, WPA, on long-term loan to the Philadelphia Museum of Art.)

Dox Thrash (Public domain, black-artists-in-the-museum.com.)

The Philadelphia Museum of Art hosted a major retrospective of Thrash's work in 2001. In a pre-show review, the *Philadelphia Inquirer* described Thrash as an artist who "refused to be confined by the moribund traditions that decreed he not depict Black female nudes and all Black subjects must be portrayed as happy individuals who like to sing and dance."

THIS USED TO BE: Home of Dox Thrash

NOW IT'S: Empty lot

LOCATION: North Central Philadelphia

"Would America Be America without Her Negro People?"

In the late 1800s, Philadelphia had one of the country's largest concentrations of African American residents, many of whom were treated as second-class citizens even decades after slavery had been abolished. Sociologist/Civil Rights activist W.E.B. Du Bois moved to the city to find out why.

Du Bois, of mixed race, grew up in a Massachusetts town where Blacks and whites lived, studied, worked, and worshipped side by side. Still, he realized that some of his schoolmates looked down on him because of his dark skin. He later wrote that "Once or twice I became painfully aware that some human beings even thought it a crime."

After earning his PhD from Harvard University, Du Bois took a job at the University of Pennsylvania. He moved into a home at the corner of South 6th and South Streets as he undertook a survey of the surrounding neighborhood's African American residents, seeking to document their lives and challenges in the hopes of finding ways to help the community. The result was *The Philadelphia Negro: A Social Study*, a landmark work that further established Du Bois as one of the great intellectuals of his time.

The mural on the building's south side is called *Mapping Courage: Honoring W.E.B. Du Bois and Engine 11.* Du Bois is pictured on the left, his neighborhood survey un-scrolling to form the street the firefighters stand upon. Engine 11 was the African American fire station. Its recruits were called "leather lungs" as they often undertook the most dangerous work.

A mural on the other side of Philadelphia Fire Department's Engine 11 depicts Du Bois with his groundbreaking work. (Photo by Tricia Pompilio.)

W.E.B. Du Bois cofounded the NAACP. (Retrieved from the Library of Congress. https://www.loc.gov/pictures/item/2003681451/.)

Du Bois posed the question, "Would America have been America without her Negro people?" He was a cofounder of the National Association for the Advancement of Colored People (NAACP) and editor of its monthly magazine. One of his most memorable quotes is "Either America will destroy ignorance, or ignorance will destroy the United States."

THIS USED TO BE: Home of W.E.B. Dubois

NOW IT'S: Philadelphia Fire Department's Engine 11

LOCATION: Bella Vista

"A Four-Star General in the Battle for Righteousness"

In 1943, 16-year-old C. DeLores Tucker protested outside a Philadelphia hotel which refused to rent rooms to African American athletes. In 1965, she joined Martin Luther King Jr.'s voting rights march from Selma to Montgomery, AL. In the 1970s, she rose to become Secretary of the Commonwealth of Pennsylvania and the first African American in Pennsylvania history to hold a cabinet post. She used that platform to advocate for passage of the Equal Rights Amendment and lowering the voting age to 18.

Tucker, who died in 2005 at age 78, lived in this home for 47 years. At her funeral, former Vice President Al Gore remembered her as "a four-star general in the battle for righteousness."

Tucker grew up on a farm outside of Philadelphia, one of 11 children born to a minister father and a mother who described herself as a "Christian feminist." She was the only African American student in her ninth-grade class. The other students called her "Black Beauty."

"I didn't take it as a compliment, it being the name of a horse," she said in a 1975 interview.

Tucker was unsuccessful in multiple runs for elected office but had political influence at both the state and national level. She made *Ebony* magazine's list of the most influential Black Americans five times, was once declared to be the best suited to be US ambassador to the UN by the National Women's Political Caucus, and is mentioned in Hillary Clinton's book *It Takes a Village*, which shares a vision of a multicultural coalition of Americans working toward a common goal.

At Tucker's funeral in North Philadelphia, Rev. Jesse Jackson Sr. remembered her as part of a "generation that changed America."

C. DeLores Tucker was a tireless advocate for women. (Public domain, thoughtco.com.)

C. DeLores Tucker, a graduate of Temple University and The Wharton School, was a Civil Rights champion who participated in the 1965 march in Selma, Alabama with Dr. Martin Luther King Jr. (Public domain, m.facebook.com/PALegislativeBlack Caucus.)

In the 1990s, Tucker took on the musical genre "gangsta rap," saying that it was degrading to women and promoted violence. She organized protests outside record stores throughout the United States. She told the *Philadelphia Inquirer* in 1980 that she planned to fight for what she thought was right "'til God stills my tongue." She did.

THIS USED TO BE: Home of C. DeLores Tucker

NOW IT'S: Private Residence

LOCATION: West Mt. Airy

The President of the Underground Railroad

Abolitionist Robert Purvis risked his life and property to help enslaved Africans find freedom. He also used his considerable fortune to advance the Women's Suffrage movement and to support Prohibition. As his 1898 obituary in *The New York Times* observed when he died at age 87, "His life was frequently in jeopardy from mobs, but, being the possessor of a strong moral and physical nature, he was undismayed and continued to follow the trend of his convictions."

Purvis was of mixed race, the son of a British cotton merchant and a free-born woman of Moroccan-Jewish descent. He was light skinned but shunned suggestions that he "pass" as white. He was 17 when he gave his first public speech against slavery.

Purvis and his two brothers inherited $250,000—the equivalent of $7 million in today's dollars—after their father's death. Purvis dedicated most of his share to his favorite causes. He cofounded the Pennsylvania Anti-Slavery Society, aiding in the construction of its headquarters, Pennsylvania Hall. Slavery supporters burned the building to the ground less than a week after its unveiling.

Purvis was often called the "president of the Underground Railroad," meaning "his house, horses, carriages, and his personal attendance, were ever at the service of travelers on that road," his obituary said.

Robert Purvis's son, Charles, was also quite accomplished. He was one of the first university-trained African American doctors. He served in the Union Army during the Civil War and worked with Howard University to establish its medical school. In 1881, he treated President James Garfield for two gunshot wounds received from a would-be assassin.

Robert Purvis was 17 when he gave his first public speech denouncing slavery. (Public domain, nps.gov)

Purvis was waiting outside his home and holding a gun when an angry pro-slavery mob arrived in 1842. (Photo by Tricia Pompilio.)

In 1842, African Americans celebrating the anniversary of slavery's end in the British West Indies were attacked by a group of mostly Irish immigrants. The angry mob made its way to Purvis's home to find him on his front porch with a gun in hand. A Catholic priest intervened, and the situation ended without violence.

Purvis later estimated that he'd helped at least one enslaved person escape to freedom every day from 1831 to 1861, about 9,000 people.

THIS USED TO BE: Home of Robert Purvis

NOW IT'S: Private residence under construction

LOCATION: Spring Garden

"An Ornament to the City"

When the American Presbyterian Church decided to build a headquarters in Philadelphia in the late 1880s, it wanted a structure that was "an ornament to the city, a fit exponent of the strength and capacity of the Presbyterian church, and a centre of beneficent power and religious influence for the elevation and enlightenment of the whole country." The result was the Witherspoon Building, which remains a jaw-droppingly ornate high-rise.

The church spent more than $1 million—about $25 million in today's dollars—on this building, hiring young architect Joseph M. Huston, who would later design the Pennsylvania State Capitol in Harrisburg. Huston wanted to "tell the story of the Organization of the Presbyterian Church in this country in Architecture, Painting and Sculpture," which is why he hired notable artists including Thomas Eakins, Alexander Stirling Calder, and Samuel Murray for the project. The 16 larger-than-life statues that adorned the building depicted biblical prophets and fathers of the American Presbyterian church. Ornate, carved medallions, still in place today, stud the structure.

The building was named to honor Rev. John Witherspoon, first president of Princeton University and the only Presbyterian clergyman to sign the Declaration of Independence.

Engraved above the building's main entrance on Juniper Street are the words "Presbyterian Board of Publication and Sabbath School Works." It also housed church offices, a library and museum, the historical society, meeting rooms, and a 1,200-seat concert hall.

The church sold the building in 1973. It is now office and retail space.

The 16 statues removed from the building's facade are now in the courtyard of the Presbyterian Historical Society, 425 Lombard Street, and are easily seen through its fence.

The American Presbyterian Church wanted a headquarters that was "an ornament to the city." (Image courtesy of Rand, McNally & Co.)

Side entrance to former Presbyterian Church headquarters. (Photo by Tricia Pompilio.)

THIS USED TO BE: American Presbyterian Church Headquarters

NOW IT'S: Mixed-use building with offices, retail and restaurant

LOCATION: Center City

Telegraph Game Changer STOP

Union Telegraph Company was a communications game-changer when it began operations in the mid-1800s, allowing people on opposite sides of the country—and eventually the world—to send and receive messages first within days, then within hours and minutes.

The first telegrams were sent via Morse code until that was replaced by teletypewriter and telex lines. The messages were then delivered to recipients via courier. Senders paid by the word, so brevity was the key, meaning verbs were often dropped. Punctuation cost extra, but the word STOP did not, so that was often how sentences ended.

News of some of the biggest events of the twentieth century was first shared via telegram: The Wright brothers sent their father one from Kitty Hawk, NC, in 1903 after their first successful flight. On April 15, 1912, the R.M.S. *Titanic* sent an emergency appeal from the North Atlantic to its New York offices: "SOS. from M. G. Y. We have struck iceberg sinking fast come to our assistance." One of the ship's survivors only had $1.25 when he safely landed in New York, and he used most of it to send his mother a one-word message: "Safe."

Western Union built this Philadelphia headquarters in 1923. It was originally four stories and featured a "telephone room" with 70 operators taking incoming messages. At its peak in 1929, Western Union processed 200 million telegrams.

The company sold the building in the 1990s. It sat unchanged for about twenty years until a massive redesign added eight stories to the building, and it reopened as condominiums in 2008.

Western Union delivered its last telegram in 2006. Two months later, Twitter CEO Jack Dorsey sent the first Tweet.

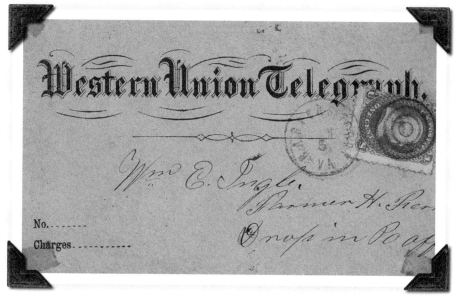

A 2015 article froM atlasobscura.com said this about Western Union: "For 150 years, the world's greatest joys, deepest condolences and proudest successes had been hand delivered within their iconic yellow envelopes, written in its own distinctive brief prose. (Western Union telegraph envelope. [Between 1861 and 1865] Photograph. Retrieved from the Library of Congress, www.loc.gov/item/2013645798/.)

Today Western Union is in the money transfer business. In 2018, the company processed more than 800 million transactions.

THIS USED TO BE: Western Union

NOW IT'S: Condominiums with retail and restaurant space

LOCATION: Center City

Private Safes! Burglar-Proof Vaults!

Entry to the Philadelphia World's Fair in 1876 was "50 cents, payable in one note." Two people could not enter with a single dollar, nor could someone get in by paying two quarters. To accommodate visitors, branches of the Centennial National Bank stood near each of the fairground's entrances. The bank's headquarters, at 31st and Market Streets, now houses Drexel University's Paul Peck Alumni Center.

The International Exhibition of Arts, Manufacturers, and Products of Soil and Mine celebrated the 100th anniversary of American independence while showcasing the country's best and brightest. One of those was architect Frank Furness, who designed Centennial National Bank's main building by mixing Victorian and Gothic architectural design elements. The red brick structure featuring a three-sided front facade topped by a clock tower was unlike any other building, not only at the fairgrounds but in the city. The sign above the entrance promised "Private safes in burglar proof vaults for rent," a boast that would appear in the bank's print advertisements in the decades that followed.

The building would continue to be used for banking for more than 70 years. Drexel purchased it in the 1970s and subdivided the interior into offices.

In 2000, the university invested $4 million to restore the building to its original state, removing the drop ceilings and layers of paint to reveal ceiling mosaics, terra cotta trim, and brilliant glass tiles. As its National

Drexel's mascot is the dragon. The bronze dragon sculpture near the Alumni Center is called Mario the Magnificent to honor an alum who reportedly did not miss a single Drexel home basketball game in 25 years.

Frank Furness designed this building as a bank for the 1876 World's Fair. It is now owned by Drexel University. (Photo by Tricia Pompilio.)

Register of Historic Places application notes, "This bank is a significant work of architecture, one of the major surviving works of Frank Furness, one of the major examples of Victorian architecture in Philadelphia and one of the best pieces of architecture in West Philadelphia."

THIS USED TO BE: Centennial National Bank

NOW IT'S: Drexel University's Paul Peck Alumni Center

LOCATION: West Philadelphia

Presidents Spoke and Slept Here

The six-story Continental Hotel was considered one of world's finest when it opened its doors in 1860. Designed by the same architect who'd conceived of Philadelphia's City Hall, it had 700 rooms and one of the country's first elevators. Presidents Ulysses S. Grant and Andrew Johnson were two of the notables who slept there. In 1861, President-Elect Abraham Lincoln addressed a crowd from one of the hotel's balconies.

Still, by the 1920s, the Continental was considered dated. (Historic preservation just wasn't a thing back then.) It was torn down and replaced by the 18-story Benjamin Franklin Hotel in 1925. Developers said the hotel was so named because it stood at the same site where Franklin, inventor and Founding Father, had "discovered" electricity and lightning were the same when he experimented with a kite and a key.

The new hotel was even more elaborate than its predecessor, with vaulted ceilings covered in reliefs; a restaurant offering martinis for 70 cents; the Crystal Ballroom, which would host hundreds of weddings in the years to follow; and more than 65,000 yards of carpet—enough to cover two city blocks. More than 1,000 people attended the gala celebrating its unveiling, which featured two orchestras, two Spanish dancers, and an opera singer, the *Philadelphia Inquirer* reported.

In 1947, the hotel made national news when it refused a room to Brooklyn Dodger Jackie Robinson. The entire team moved to another facility.

The building was converted to apartments with retail shops and offices in the 1980s. It was unveiled as the luxury Franklin Residences in 2014 after a $13 million renovation.

You can see the building's interior in the 2012 movie *Silver Linings Playbook*. The Crystal Ballroom hosts the dance competition in the film's finale.

Abraham Lincoln addressed a crowd from a Continental Hotel balcony in 1861. (Images courtesy of the Library Company of Philadelphia.)

THIS USED TO BE: Continental/Benjamin Franklin Hotel

NOW IT'S: Residences at the Franklin

LOCATION: Center City

"One of the Greatest Institutions . . . in Philadelphia"

Shibe Park set the standard for twentieth-century ballparks when it was unveiled in April 1909. It was the first concrete and steel stadium in major league baseball, with grandstand seating for 23,000. On its opening day, Philadelphia Mayor John Reyburn proclaimed it "one of the greatest institutions in the bounds of Philadelphia . . . the finest baseball stadium in the country," the *Philadelphia Inquirer* reported. "The park is a masterpiece. . . . In the future all visitors will want to be directed to Twenty-second Street and Lehigh Avenue."

The Philadelphia Athletics, led by manager Connie Mack, won the World Series in 1910, 1911, and 1913. Besides fans in the stands, the Athletics were cheered by hundreds of people perched on residential rooftops who'd paid homeowners for the opportunity. The team eventually built a 50-foot-tall barrier, known as the Spite Fence, to block views of the field from neighboring homes.

In the 1930s, Shibe Park hosted its first night game and became the home field for the city's other baseball team, the Phillies, as well as its football team, the Eagles. In the 1940s, it underwent further expansion, replacing stairs with ramps, adding a restaurant, and installing a new scoreboard.

Mack, who began managing the Athletics in 1901, stayed on the job for 50 years. He was the first manager to win the World Series three times. The stadium was renamed in his honor in 1953. In the five years that followed, the Athletics moved to California and the Eagles moved to Franklin Field, leaving the Phillies as the park's only team.

The Phillies have called Citizens Bank Park on South Broad Street home since 2004. The Eagles play at neighboring Lincoln Financial Field.

Deliverance Evangelistic Church, built in 1992, resembles a stadium. (Photo by Tricia Pompilio.)

As the stadium aged and the neighborhood around it deteriorated, city officials decided to build the Phillies and Eagles a new home field in South Philadelphia. The once cutting-edge ballfield hosted its last game in October 1970. It was razed in 1976.

Deliverance Evangelistic Church built a new 5,000-seat facility on the site in 1992. The megachurch resembles a ballpark.

THIS USED TO BE: Shibe Park/Connie Mack Stadium

NOW IT'S: Deliverance Evangelistic Church

LOCATION: Fishtown

The High Priestess of American Musicians

In 1905, young Marian Anderson was walking to the grocery store when she saw a piece of paper in the street. It was a handbill advertising her upcoming church singing debut. As she later recalled, "I picked it up, and there in a corner was my picture with my name under it. 'Come hear the baby contralto, 10 years old,' it said. I was actually eight. What excitement!"

The legendary singer and her many notable achievements have since inspired generations. In 1939, after a concert hall refused to book her because of the color of her skin, Anderson performed in front of the Lincoln Memorial, with 75,000 people in attendance and millions more listening on the radio. In 1955, she was the first African American singer to perform at the Metropolitan Opera.

Internationally-acclaimed opera singer Jessye Norman, who is also African-American, recalled how she felt when, at age 10, she first heard a recording of Anderson's voice: "I listened, thinking 'This cannot just be a voice, so rich and beautiful.' It was a revelation. And I wept."

Anderson sang at the inaugurations of Presidents Dwight Eisenhower and John F. Kennedy. She toured internationally, taking a 10-week-long tour of India and the Far East on behalf of the US State Department. As a 1989 article in *The New York Times* noted, "Miss Anderson's place as a high priestess of American musicians, whatever their color, is not to be denied."

Anderson's childhood debut was at the Church of the Crucifixion, located at 620 South 8th Street. It is the second-oldest African American Episcopal Church in Pennsylvania.

Portrait of Marian Anderson by Carl Van Vechten, 1940. (Retrieved from the Library of Congress //hdl.loc.gov/loc.pnp/van.5a51648.)

Marian Anderson was the first Black woman to perform at the Metropolitan Opera House. (Photo by Tricia Pompilio.)

The music legend, who died in 1993 at age 96, purchased this home in 1924. It is now a museum devoted to telling her story through photos, memorabilia, clothing, books, and films.

THIS USED TO BE: Home of Marian Anderson

NOW IT'S: Marian Anderson Residence Museum

LOCATION: Graduate Hospital

A Sound Like No Other

"The Sound of Philadelphia"—funky soul with layers of vocals and orchestral arrangements featuring horns and strings—was born at Sigma Sound Studios. Engineer Joe Tarsia, who founded the studio in 1968, described the sound as "Black music in a tuxedo," telling the Associated Press, "I loved trying to create a sound bigger than the environment it's in. I was a fan of the lush, big, open sounds."

Producers/songwriters Kenny Gamble and Leon Huff—of Philadelphia International Records fame—and Thom Bell worked with Aretha Franklin, Teddy Pendergrass, The Spinners, and The Stylistics.

Sigma Sound Studios as it looked in 1979. (Photo by Arthur Stoppe. Image courtesy of the Preservation Alliance of Greater Philadelphia.)

Among the hit songs recorded here: The Trammps' "Disco Inferno," The O'Jays' "Love Train," McFadden and Whitehead's "Ain't No Stoppin' Us Now," and The Three Degrees' "When Will I See You Again?"

In 1974, David Bowie and a band that included vocalist Luther Vandross recorded parts of the *Young Americans* album at Sigma. "What was unique about it was that he came to Sigma for something that Philadelphia had," Tarsia told the *Philadelphia Inquirer* in 2016. "He wanted that sound."

Only the studio's exterior remains, the interior gutted years ago.

Visit the former home of Philadelphia International Records at 309 South Broad Street. The Philadelphia Music Alliance's Walk of Fame runs on South Broad Street between Walnut and Locust Streets.

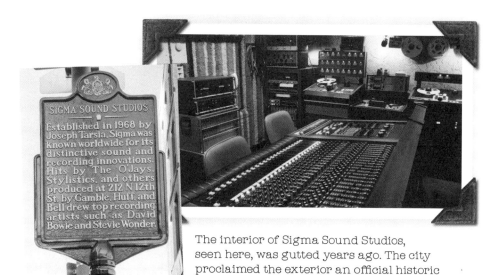

The interior of Sigma Sound Studios, seen here, was gutted years ago. The city proclaimed the exterior an official historic site in 2015. It is as yet undeveloped.

(Images courtesy of Sigma Sound Studio Records, SCRC 212, Special Collections Research Center, Temple University Libraries, Philadelphia, Pennsylvania.)

THIS USED TO BE: Sigma Sound Studio

NOW IT'S: Empty Building

LOCATION: Chinatown

From Hoop Skirts to War Work

In 1820, English immigrant Abednego Moore noted the following in his new company ledger: "Fifty-five and one-half pounds of Bonnet Wire." And with that sale, the Philadelphia Insulated Wire company was born.

In its earliest days, the business provided cloth-covered wire for use in women's clothing, including hoop skirts and corsets. The company steadily evolved and, two decades later, Moore was supplying all of the copper wire Samuel Morse needed to send the first telegraph message from Washington to Baltimore. It was also one of the first companies in the US to produce waterproof cable.

The company's original building—and most of its records—was destroyed by fire in 1900. The current five-story brick structure was completed a year later. The business, then led by Abednego Moore's grandson, Alfred Fitler Moore, continued to grow as the country became electrified. During World War II, Philadelphia Insulated Wire produced millions of yards of wire for military use.

The Moores helmed the company for more than a century. Its legacy includes the Moore College of Art & Design, which was renamed after a family member gave the all-female institution $3 million, and the University of Pennsylvania's Moore College of Electrical Engineering, launched with a $1.5 million donation from the family.

The latter is famed as the birthplace of the computer industry: the first programmable, general-purpose digital computer was built here in the 1940s. ENIAC—Electronic Numerical Integrator and

A quick stroll through the Old City neighborhood will reveal other former factories and warehouses that are now residential, including the K. Strauss Cigar and Cigarette, 303 North 3rd Street, and The Essex, 300 North 3rd Street, a machinery company.

The Philadelphia Insulated Wire Company provided all of the wire Samuel Moore needed to send the first telegram from Washington to Baltimore. (Photo by Tricia Pompilio.)

Computer—was introduced to the world in 1946 as "the world's fastest calculating machine," the Associated Press said, noting that "the robot possibly opened the mathematical way to better living for every man."

This building was converted to condominiums in the early 1990s.

THIS USED TO BE: Philadelphia Insulated Wire Company

NOW IT'S: Wireworks - Condominiums

LOCATION: Old City

Wilbur: The Buds Came First

The growing popularity of rail travel led to an unexpected demand in another industry: The candy business.

Partners Henry Oscar Wilbur and Samuel Croft joined forces in 1865 to manufacture and sell molasses and hard candies on passenger trains. The confectionary industry wasn't that high tech back then: As the Wilbur Chocolate Co.'s website notes, all one needed was "a kettle, with a coal or coke fire, some buckets and a marble slab."

The company soon added chocolate and cocoa to its product lines. In 1884, Wilbur and Croft parted ways. Croft took the hard candy business. Wilbur took his chances on chocolate, calling his business H.O. Wilbur & Sons and building this factory in 1887. It is the second oldest chocolate company in the United States.

One of the company's signature products, both then and now, is the Wilbur Bud, small pieces of chocolate that resemble flowers. They were originally sold individually wrapped in foil. The Buds debuted in 1894, "around the same time another Pennsylvania-based chocolate manufacturer began producing a copycat drop product that's still foil wrapped today," the company website notes.

Generations of Wilbur family members dedicated themselves to the business, studying the art of chocolate making in Germany and France. A third generation of the Wilbur family developed the machine that foil-wrapped the Buds.

Philadelphia was a confectionary hub for more than a century. Whitman's made candy history with the introduction of its Whitman Sampler, which was packed with a consumer-friendly key identifying each chocolate piece.

H.O. Wilbur & Sons is the second oldest chocolate company in the United States. (Photo by Tricia Pompilio.)

A Wilbur's chocolate ad from 1911 featuring the Bud. (Public domain, pinterest.com.)

In the 1920s, one section of the factory was sacrificed for construction of the Benjamin Franklin Bridge over the Delaware River to New Jersey. The company left the city for the suburbs in the 1930s. Wilbur is now owned by Cargill and boasts of the freshness of their product that goes "From Bean to Bud."

THIS USED TO BE: H.O. Wilbur & Sons Chocolate Company

NOW IT'S: Chocolate Works — Apartments

LOCATION: Old City

"The Facility . . . Is Most Remarkable"

In the 1800s, Howell & Brothers was the world's largest wallpaper company, using 2,000 tons of paper to produce six million rolls of finished wallcoverings annually. Its manufacturing plant and showroom sprawled across this two-acre lot.

The company was known for its high quality. It was the first American company to offer machine-made products and the first to print color wallpaper. An 1875 *Owensboro Examiner* article described the company in breathless terms: "In the manufacture of paper hangings Philadelphia ranks first," it gushed. "The facility . . . is most remarkable. Hundreds of rolls of blank paper can be printed . . . and be ready for the market in a few hours, and the amount produced annually by this one concern is greater than the circumference of the globe."

The next notable tenant of this building was the Frankford Candy and Chocolate Company, which remains one of the nation's biggest producers of chocolate Easter bunnies. A 1989 article in *The New York Times* observed that consumers were no longer satisfied with a hollow rabbit with a ribbon around its neck, quoting Frankford executive vice president Alan H. Kline as saying, "There was a time when a rabbit could just sit or stand. Now a rabbit has to do more."

That year, Frankford offered more than 100 different types of chocolate rabbits, including Dunkin' Don, which came with a candy basketball; Bunny Appleseed with a red candy apple; Prime Bunnerina wearing toe shoes; Huckle Bunny with a yellow candy fish; and Bunny Starhooper, an astronaut bunny accompanied by two miniature spacemen. In the 1990s, the company's rabbit mascot, known as Frankie, had his own 800 number.

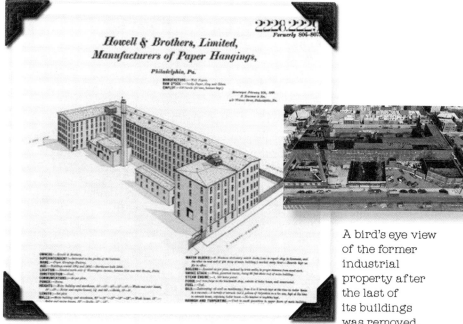

Howell & Brothers, Limited,
Manufacturers of Paper Hangings,

Philadelphia, Pa.

A bird's eye view
of the former
industrial
property after
the last of
its buildings
was removed.
(Courtesy of
Google Earth.)

Besides Howell & Brothers and the Frankford
Candy and Chocolate Company, the factory
housed the American Can Company, a furniture
warehouse. (Image courtesy of Map Collection,
Free Library of Philadelphia.)

Other products currently produced by the
Frankford Candy include marshmallow
Peeps and "Krabby Patty Sliders," a treat
inspired by *Spongebob Squarepants*.

THIS USED TO BE: Howell & Brothers Wallcovers/
Frankford Candy and Chocolate Factory

NOW IT'S: Private homes and an apartment
complex with on-site retail.

LOCATION: Gray's Ferry

From Technical School to Neighborhood Hub

When Edward W. Bok Technical High School opened in 1938, its students could choose a trade-specific course of study while still enjoying regular academic courses and extracurricular activities. There was a full kitchen for those interested in the culinary arts, an auto shop for aspiring mechanics, cosmetology classes for future spa owners, and dedicated spaces for teaching bricklaying, welding, plumbing, and plastering. City officials said Bok represented a new generation of technical education, moving beyond wood and metal classes to present career tracks that would appeal to urban youth.

At its peak, Bok had 3,000 students. Among the notable alumni: Sherman Hemsley, the actor best known for playing George Jefferson on two CBS sitcoms, and Bunny Sigler, a singer/songwriter/producer who was integral to developing the "Philly Sound" of the 1970s. When the Philadelphia School District shut the school down in 2013, there were fewer than 1,000 pupils.

The building was bought at auction in 2014. Its developers have taken what they call a "light touch" to renovations, meaning the halls are still lined with lockers, and its gymnasiums still carry with school pride banners. The eight-story, 340,000-square-foot structure is now a "maker space," home to about 150 businesses including salons, a boutique gym, offices for local artists, nonprofit organizations, a coffee shop, a ground-floor restaurant, and rooftop bar.

Bok Bar is seasonal. It has an awesome view of the city skyline.

Bok, formerly a technical high school, is now a maker space with a variety of businesses. (Photo by Tricia Pompilio.)

Members of fitness studio KG Strong make good use of the building's locker-lined hallways. (Photo by Mike Persico.)

THIS USED TO BE: Edward W. Bok Technical High School

NOW IT'S: Mixed-use building with offices, retail, restaurants, and workout facilities

LOCATION: South Philadelphia

Cheesesteaks? Ask Us about Our Tastykakes

In 1914, a baker and an egg salesman joined forces to create the Tasty Baking Company, making and selling individually-wrapped snack cakes for ten cents each. By year's end, they'd taken in $300,000, about $7.7 million today. Tastykakes had arrived.

The company grew quickly, grossing $1 million by 1918, or $17 million in today's dollars. To meet demand, Tasty Baking built a five-story factory in North Philadelphia. A short time later, it launched a product that still defines the company today: Butterscotch Krimpets. Lunch-sized fruit pies hit the market in 1930. Peanut Butter Kandy Kakes, Tasty Baking's most popular product, were introduced a year later.

In 2010, Tasty Baking closed this factory and moved into a state-of-the-art facility in South Philadelphia. Some executives worried about the change, with an executive vice president telling *The Philadelphia Daily News*, "When you're baking in those same pans for decades, and suddenly you have new, automated equipment, you have to make sure that our Krimpet still tastes like our Krimpet and our chocolate cupcake still tastes like our chocolate cupcake. Otherwise, you're in trouble."

The former factory was converted into a shopping center called Bakers Square. The neighborhood had long been a "food desert," meaning most residents were unable to get to full-size grocery stores. Bakers Square ended that. Its ShopRite has a health clinic, bank, in-store nutritionist, and a social services office.

Almost all of the current ShopRite employees come from the surrounding neighborhood. Many had struggled to find steady employment until the store arrived.

Tasty Baking Company in 1977. (Public domain, pldcphilablog.com.)

Tasty Baking's North Philadelphia factory seen before the 2010 move to the Philadelphia Navy Yard. (Public domain, pidcphilablog.com.)

THIS USED TO BE: Tasty Baking Company
NOW IT'S: Bakers Square Shopping Center
LOCATION: Nicetown

From "Sportcoats" to Senior Citizens

Fashion designer Stanley Blacker was often called "Mr. Sportcoats" and rightly so. He brought innovation to a staid product, offering new shapes, new fabrics, and new colors multiple times a year until, as a 1962 *United Press International* story noted, "a man developed an inferiority complex if he didn't have the proper jacket for the proper occasion."

Blacker worked in his family's clothing business before launching his eponymous company in 1955. It was headquartered in New York but products were manufactured in the seven-story textile factory that once stood at this corner.

Blacker was the first designer to sew his name onto his clothing and to advertise nationally, arguably creating the designer name craze. His customers were largely conservative businessmen and politicians. There were multiple Ivy Leaguers in the mix. Students at Cornell University, which has a tradition of class blazers, chose to wear Stanley Blacker in 1964, 1966, and 1967.

Blacker would unveil as many as 1,800 different styles per year, available for purchase in upscale stores across the United States. A Fall 1966 newspaper ad promoted "Rugged, bold plaids in lofty tweed effects. All wools, Dacron & wool and silk & wool . . . adroitly shaped by Stanley Blacker in 2- and 3-button models – center or side vented." An April 1977 ad promised "light, cool, comfortable . . . utterly fashionable. Stanley Blacker lush cotton sports jackets . . . in the newest checks of Navy, Green, Light blue, pink."

Stanley Blacker's Philadelphia factory closed in 1991. It was torn down and replaced by NewCourtland LIFE Center, which provides elderly individuals with activities and socializing during the day.

Boyd's Philadelphia, 1818 Chestnut Street, is the city's current go-to upscale clothing dealer. It's also included in this book, having originated as a funeral home.

The NewCourtland LIFE Center serves hundreds of seniors each day. It was developed on the footprint of the former Stanley Blacker suit factory. (Image courtesy of www. newcourtland.org.)

Stanley Blacker

(Images courtesy of StanleyBlacker.com.)

Cecil Gee introduces the classic blazer, tailored by Stanley Blacker. Steeping of a superb all wool flannel and detailed with metal buttons. Stanley Blacker Rockefeller Center, New York. U.S.A.

American sport coat designer. It is smartly cut along traditional lines.

Available at these CECIL-GEE stores.

39-45 Shaftesbury Avenue, London W1, 83-85 Brompton Road, London SW3, and branches.

THIS USED TO BE: Stanley Blacker Suit Factory

NOW IT'S: NewCourtland LIFE Center

LOCATION: Tioga

From Mr. Budd to Mrs. Kroc

Edward Budd opened his eponymous company in 1912. In its prime, it was involved in every aspect of the transportation business, from cars to trucks to subway cars to airplanes to boats to rockets. Budd was an innovator in the use of stainless steel, finding new ways to manipulate the strong, noncorrosive material.

Budd had been working for another metalworking company in the city when he decided to branch out on his own and founded the Edward G. Budd Manufacturing Company. He hired about a dozen of his former coworkers and the company's first shop "was so small it was necessary to install a large press in a rented circus tent pitched in an adjoining lot," the *Times* reported.

But the firm grew quickly. In 1914, it had 300 employees; by 1916, there were 2,000.

Budd was a bold businessman. To convince auto makers that using stainless steel was superior to making cars by mounting wood, steel, and leather to a chassis, he had an elephant stand on the roof of the car bodies he'd crafted. He dared the other designers to do the same.

During World War I, the Budd Company crafted steel helmets, mess kits, truck bodies, bombs, and shells, employing 4,700 workers by Armistice Day in 1918. During World War II, the company provided materials to every branch of the military and was the original manufacturer of the bazooka projectile and rifle grenade. By war's end the company employed more than 10,000 workers.

The Kroc Center is in the heart of a neighborhood known as Nicetown. While the residents are perfectly friendly, it's more likely that the name derives from Revolutionary War Captain John Nice, who led the patriots during the battle at nearby Germantown.

The Budd Company created products for every aspect of the transportation industry. (Public domain, pinterest.com.)

When Budd died at age 75 in 1946, his obituary in *The New York Times* summed him up this way: "A self-made man, Mr. Budd rose from a machinist's apprentice to head of the $80 million Budd Company."

The Budd Company closed its Philadelphia branch in 2003. (It still operates in Detroit.) The sprawling property has since been divided into smaller lots. A large portion of the land now houses the Salvation Army Kroc Center of Philadelphia, which opened in 2010. It features an indoor pool and water park, exercise and meeting rooms, and an education and computer center. It also offers multiple athletic fields, walking trails, and a picnic area. The center is named for the late Joan Kroc, wife of the founder of McDonald's, who gave the Salvation Army $1.5 billion to build community centers across the country.

THIS USED TO BE: Edward G. Budd Manufacturing Company

NOW IT'S: Salvation Army Kroc Center of Philadelphia

LOCATION: Nicetown

A Holy Place Replaces a Bustling Textile Mill

In the early 1800s, Philadelphia's Manayunk neighborhood was a sleepy rural village on the banks of the Schuylkill River. Less than 50 years later, it was a hive of activity, with bustling industry and constant construction to meet the growing need for housing. The difference? The construction of almost 40 mills producing paper, fabric, and yarn and an influx of hundreds of workers of all ages.

Brothers Andrew and John Flanagan were relatively late to the game when they built Freeland Mills in 1882. The company produced carpet yarns. Like many other mills along the river, it was family-owned and depended on the labor of other families for its success. Despite the passage of state laws forbidding child labor, a census of Manayunk mill workers in the late 1880s found that the labor force was almost equally divided between adults and children, with parents and children laboring side by side.

The textile mills flourished in part thanks to trade protections put in place by President William McKinley in the 1890s. The *Philadelphia Inquirer* reported that mill owners were pleased. "Mssrs. A. Flanagan and Bro. are satisfied that all the products and businesses will generally benefit. 'The numerous imported goods kept out by this bill,' they say, 'will now be made here and the country will reap all the avails.'"

Almost a century after construction, Freeland Mills was closed. It sat empty for years until the 300-family-strong congregation of Mishkan

Mishkan Shalom is a Reconstructionist/ Reconstructing Judaism congregation formed in 1988 that embraces those who may have felt invisible in other congregations, including interfaith families, those with limited means, and LGBTQ Jews.

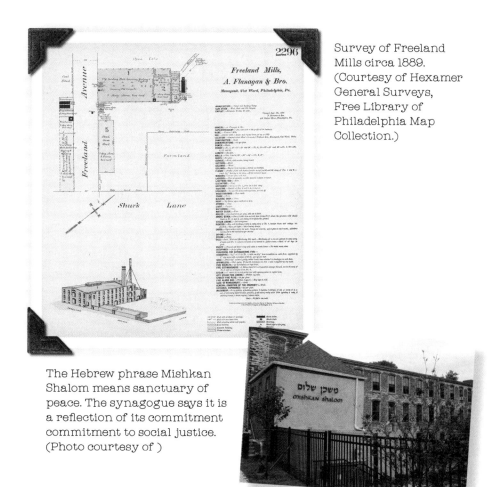

Survey of Freeland Mills circa 1889. (Courtesy of Hexamer General Surveys, Free Library of Philadelphia Map Collection.)

The Hebrew phrase Mishkan Shalom means sanctuary of peace. The synagogue says it is a reflection of its commitment commitment to social justice. (Photo courtesy of)

Shalom Synagogue purchased the property. Converting the mill into a 500-seat sanctuary with classrooms, a library, and offices took six years and cost almost $4 million. The congregation has called the old mill home since 2005.

. . . .

THIS USED TO BE: Freeland Mills

NOW IT'S: Mishkan Shalom Synagogue

LOCATION: Manayunk

. . . .

A Neighborhood Ornament, Restored

Rave reviews for Germantown's St. Peter's Episcopal Church began before the church had even hosted its first sermon. The Gothic stone structure, designed by renowned architects Frank Furness and George Hewitt, was called "quite an ornament to the neighborhood" by the *Philadelphia Inquirer* in December 1873. The article went on to describe the church's "beautiful corona of gas lights," the chestnut pews and walnut furniture, the handsome stained glass and spire "surmounted with a wrought iron cross in blue and gold." The church's opening, miles from downtown Philadelphia, coincided with the expansion of the local rail system.

For more than a century, St. Peter's was a neighborhood focal point, facing the main thoroughfare but seemingly apart from the hubbub thanks to the two-acre lot it shared with its chapel and parish house.

But as has happened in cities across the country, the church's membership dwindled. Unable to keep up with the aging building's rising maintenance costs, the church hosted its final service in April 2005.

The buildings stood empty and neglected for years, much to the distress of locals. In 2013, a developer purchased the property and invested $4 million to create a new campus for the Waldorf School of Philadelphia, an independent, private institution serving students in pre-K through eighth grade.

The school settled into its new home in September 2015.

The Waldorf School's teachings are based on the education philosophy of Rudolf Steiner, who aimed to develop the pupils' intellectual, artistic, and practical skills in an integrated and holistic manner.

St. Peter's Episcopal Church today. (Image courtesy of the Waldorf School of Philadelphia.)

THIS USED TO BE: St. Peter's Episcopal Church

NOW IT'S: The Waldorf School of Philadelphia

LOCATION: Germantown

The What . . . ?

Most locals don't know that the high-rise at the intersection of North Broad Street and Erie Avenue was built for the National Bank of North Philadelphia. They're unaware that it's officially called the Beury Building, named after the bank's first president, Charles Beury, who also served as president of Temple University.

Most folks just call it the "Boner 4Ever" building. Those are the words you'll see written vertically for five floors starting near the top when you drive north on North Broad Street.

And if you're coming south? That side reads "Forever Boner."

It's unclear when those words were written on the crumbling, windowless structure, which has sat empty for the last 40 years, and that is a shame because it all began with such promise. The 11-story skyscraper—topped by a three-story penthouse with a pyramid roof—was completed in 1927. It is the only Art Deco–style building outside of the downtown area.

The bank didn't last long so the building welcomed other businesses. During World War II, part of the building was a designated bomb shelter that could hold up to 2,600 people. It also housed the city's rationing board.

In 1950, the Selective Service moved in. Other businesses, including at least one insurance company, did as well.

And then . . . ? Empty.

In the 1980s, the city attempted to buy the building but failed. In the 1990s, the building's owner went to jail for hiring unskilled homeless people to remove asbestos from the structure.

Mural Arts Philadelphia did a similarly styled painting on both sides of the building at 2701 North Broad Street. Traveling south, 40-foot-tall letters read "RISE." Heading south, 80-foot-tall letters read "SHINE."

The graffiti on the Beury Building is how many locals know the building. (Photo by Tricia Pompilio.)

In 2012, a new developer stepped in and purchased the structure. The current plan, announced in early 2020, is to convert the Beury Building into a hotel with a restaurant and retail shops on the lower floors. The project's interior designer told the *Philadelphia Inquirer* that planners would like to incorporate the graffiti into the final renovation.

That's good news for Philadelphians, including the Twitter user who bemoaned the possible loss of this landmark: "Boner 4Ever was one of the few good things left in this world."

THIS USED TO BE: National Bank of North Philadelphia

NOW IT'S: Empty Building

LOCATION: Hunting Park

A Watery Work of Art

More than 5,000 Philadelphians died when yellow fever swept through the city in the late 1700s and the smell of death and decay lingered for months afterward. In response, local leaders decided to find a way to bring fresh water into the city to clean the streets and promote healthier living.

The first pump house of the Fairmount Waterworks opened near City Hall in 1801, using steam engines to collect water from the Schuylkill River in an 18,000-gallon wooden tank before distributing it to the homes and businesses of paying customers. As demand for clean water grew, the city unveiled the larger Fairmount Water Works in 1815, storing the collected water in a three-million-gallon earthen reservoir on land now occupied by the Philadelphia Museum of Art. The system's engine room occupied the neoclassical building that remains today.

The Fairmount Water Works served as a model for the nation. In the 1820s, engineers eliminated the need for unreliable steam engines by damming the river and harvesting its power using water wheels. At the same time, the city landscaped the nearby grounds, built riverside paths, and dotted the banks with sculptures.

According to the 1976 application to the National Register of Historic Places for the structure: "The Water Works became one of Philadelphia's best known sites and its citizens' favorite promenade. This blending of new technology with old landscape and the cultivation of that natural scenery was a self-confident expression of man's peaceful, beneficial mastery of nature."

It also notes that, "Charles Dickens, critical of everything American, found the Water Works at Fairmount beautiful."

The city developed a new system for securing water in 1909. In the years since, the building has housed an aquarium, a public indoor pool, and a bar and restaurant.

The Schuylkill River hosts major rowing events, including the Dad Vail Regatta, the Head of the Schuylkill, and an annual Dragon Boat Festival.

Built in 1815, the Fairmount Water Works was built to provide fresh water to citizens. (Photo by Tricia Pompilio.)

THIS USED TO BE: Philadelphia Water Department Pumping Station

NOW IT'S: WaterWorks Event Space

LOCATION: Art Museum

"A Fitting Monument to Our Employees"

The Provident Mutual Life Insurance Company was one of the country's largest in the early 1900s. Founded by Quaker businessmen in 1865, the firm was originally housed in a cramped building in Center City. Like so many people and companies that had come before it, when they needed more room, the owners decided to head west.

Provident Mutual purchased 13 acres that had been part of the campus of the Institute of Pennsylvania Hospital, a.k.a. Kikbride's Hospital, a.k.a. Pennsylvania Hospital for Mental and Nervous Diseases. It hired the Boston firm of Cram and Ferguson to design its new home. Lead architect Ralph Adams Cram, who was so well known that he was featured on the cover of *Time* magazine in 1926, was famous for his neoclassical and Gothic Revival designs.

The new headquarters, completed in 1928 at a cost of $3 million, equivalent to $44 million in today's dollars, featured a golden dome and stately clock tower topped by a ship-shaped weathervane. One executive said it was "a fitting monument to the work of the employees." The campus had an indoor pool, auditorium, baseball field, and tennis courts. Employees could enjoy free lunch every day in the company cafeteria.

The company grew steadily, doubling in size by the 1960s. Still, Provident Mutual moved out of West Philadelphia in 1983. Multiple

Before its move to West Philadelphia, the bank and insurance company were located in a Frank Furness–designed building at Chestnut and South 4th Streets. Some architecture insiders say that the structure was Furness's greatest work. It was demolished in 1959.

Before Provident Mutual Life Insurance constructed this building, this lot was home to the Pennsylvania Hospital for Mental and Nervous Diseases. (Photo by Tricia Pompilio.)

attempts at repurposing its former campus fell through in the following decades. The land is now slated to be redeveloped for the use of the University of Pennsylvania, Children's Hospital of Pennsylvania, Public Health Care Management Corp, and the YWCA.

THIS USED TO BE: Provident Mutual Life Insurance Company

NOW IT'S: Future Health and Wellness Campus

LOCATION: West Philadelphia

You Know this Artist's Work, if Not His Name

When Frank Gasparro told people he worked as a sculptor, the follow-up question inevitably was, "Where can I see your work?" Gasparro's reply always puzzled them.

"In your pocket," he'd say.

Gasparro, who died in 2001 at age 92, was an engraver for the US Mint for almost 40 years, holding the title of chief engraver from 1965 until his retirement in 1981. His best-known work: The tails side of the Lincoln penny, which between 1959 and 2008 featured Gasparro's interpretation of the Lincoln Memorial. The life long Philadelphian lived in the house that once stood here.

The young Gasparro always wanted to be an artist, to his musician father's chagrin. The older man originally tried to discourage the boy by throwing out his drawings. He eventually let young Frank hone his craft with free art classes at the Graphic Sketch Club—now the Samuel S. Fleischer Art Memorial, 719 Catharine St. Gasparro, who studied sculpture with an artist who had assisted Auguste Rodin, excelled as a student at the Pennsylvania Academy of Fine Arts.

Gasparro then joined the US Mint as a junior engraver in 1942. In 1959, the Mint decided to mark the 150th anniversary of Lincoln's birth by releasing a penny with a new tails side to replace the existing "wheat ears." Gasparro's design was one of more than 20 proposals submitted by

Look carefully at Gasparro's penny design. Between the sixth and seventh columns of the Lincoln Memorial is a hint of the statue that sits inside of it. Mint officials originally asked him to remove that touch, saying it looked like a smudge. Gasparro said the building looked like a library without it.

Gasparro's Lincoln penny featuring the Lincoln statue between the sixth and seventh columns of the Lincoln Memorial. (Public domain, usacoinbook.com.)

Frank Gasparro, 10th chief engraver and sculptor of the US Mint, designing the "tails" side of the Kennedy half-dollar. (Public domain, usacoinbook.com.)

Mint artists. For the rest of his life Gasparro spoke about how honored he was to have his design chosen. In his *Washington Post* obituary, a former Mint colleague noted that Gasparro "never walked by a penny on the street. He'd always pick it up—that's personal, baby."

Gasparro also designed both sides of the Dwight D. Eisenhower and the Susan B. Anthony dollars, and the tails side of the Kennedy half dollar.

THIS USED TO BE: Home of Frank Gasparro

NOW IT'S: Empty Lot

LOCATION: Bella Vista

The Pennsylvania Railroad's "Chinese Wall"

Philadelphia was a battleground during the Golden Age of Railroads, with the Pennsylvania and Reading Railroad companies often engaged in a game of one-upmanship. In 1881, PRR was the first company to open a downtown terminal—unfortunately, any feelings of victory soon disappeared.

PRR's Broad Street Station included a five-story Victorian Gothic building set up for offices, waiting areas, and a double train shed with nine tracks on which 160 trains came and went daily. As more regional rails came online, the building became uncomfortably crowded. Five years after the station opened, PRR hired architect Frank Furness's firm to design a larger one.

The architects proposed an expanded concourse and an elevated stone viaduct stretching almost a mile between City Hall and the Schuylkill River. Open arches would allow north-south transit on the numbered streets. More than 200 buildings were torn down to construct the soon-to-be-despised structure called the "Chinese Wall."

As the PhillyHistory.org blog eloquently noted, the viaduct "severely hindered physical access from Center City to North Philadelphia.

Each one of its archways was a dark, stinking cavern, usually filled with refuse. . . . Surrounding real estate, especially on Market and Arch

The Reading Railroad's buildings are still an important part of the city. Its headhouse is the main entrance to the Pennsylvania Convention Center while the train shed is the convention center's Grand Hall and ballroom. The jewel left behind is Reading Terminal Market, an enclosed food and souvenir showcase and food court that has become one of the city's most beloved attractions.

Different views of the original Pennsylvania Railroad Station, also known as Broad Street Station between 1881 and 1953. (Public domain, facebook.com/oldimagesofphiladelphia/.)

streets, suffered. The steam trains belched black smoke at all hours of the day and night, soiling surrounding buildings with soot and choking the air with fumes."

Things got worse for the PRR when the Reading Railroad opened its new passenger station and headhouse a few blocks away. Headlines in the January 30, 1893, *Philadelphia Inquirer* recorded the Reading's victorious opening this way: "The First Train Departed Yesterday Amidst the Cheers of Spectators," "Scenes in in the Big Depot: Everything Works Smoothly and Punctually."

Broad Street Station and the "Chinese Wall" were torn down in 1953. The PRR declared bankruptcy in 1970.

THIS USED TO BE: Broad Street Station

NOW IT'S: Center City Philadelphia

LOCATION: Center City

Looking up from Upholstery

New York–based B.L. Solomon's Sons built the Orinoka Mills Corporation in the 1880s. The company specialized in upholstery fabrics and "artistic furniture." This five-story factory produced woven silk fabric and curtains as well as sturdier furniture coverings which were sold in Solomon's Sons' New York showroom. An 1878 *New York Times* article said that the company's Manhattan display windows featured "a suit of furniture upholstered with an entirely new material called 'Toile Imprime.'" The piece also gushed over the "magnificent establishment" where "are found the various styles of cloth used for upholstering purposes, from which the head of a family with an economical turn of mind may select a pattern and have his old furniture re-covered."

By 1913, the company's 300 looms produced wool, worsted, and cotton furniture coverings. Its products were of such high quality that some are still available for sale today, second-, third-, or even fourth-hand. The factory closed in the 1980s when the business was purchased by a North Carolina textile company that also acquired its priceless 10,000-piece fabric library.

The business's closure and the loss of jobs were a blow to an already struggling neighborhood. A quote from a 2016 *Next City* article describes those years in this way: "Linda Mottolo remembers when her brother worked at Orinoka Mills back in the 1980s. She also remembers a decade later, long after the jobs vanished, when her daughter would break into the shuttered factory building to shoot heroin."

The Kensington neighborhood is one of Philadelphia's "river wards," all of which were severely hurt by the loss of manufacturing jobs in the city. It is now one of the city's most dynamic neighborhoods, bustling with new homes and businesses.

Orinoka Civic House offers apartments for low-to-moderate income residents. (Photo by Tricia Pompilio.)

In 2015, after years of inactivity, the New Kensington Community Development Corporation began an $18 million rehab of the old factory. It reopened two years later with apartments for low-to-moderate-income residents, offices for the nonprofit organization, and more than 7,500 square feet of commercial and retail space.

THIS USED TO BE: Orinoka Mills

NOW IT'S: Orinoka Civic House

LOCATION: Kensington

"If You Think You Can Build a Better Car . . ."

This section of North Broad Street was once known as Automobile Row, a reference to the many car showrooms, repair shops, parts suppliers, and manufacturers that filled these blocks. The Ford Motor Company's massive building in the 2700 block of North Broad Street marked the row's northern border, while the Gomery-Schwartz Autocar Company at 130 North Broad Street served as the southern border. In between rose the eight-story Packard Motor Corporation building at 315-21 North Broad Street.

Packard was one of the country's premiere luxury car brands, building its first vehicle in 1899. Brothers James and William Packard were inspired to start their own company after spending $1,000 on a new Winton automobile that broke down during the 70-mile drive between Winton's Cleveland plant and the brothers' central Ohio home. When they complained to the company's president, he allegedly said, "If you think you can build a better car, why don't you try?"

So they did, and they were successful. (Have you heard of the Winton brand?) Within a decade, Packard was expanding, building plants and showrooms throughout the country. Detroit-based Albert Kahn, one of the country's best-known industrial architects, designed Philadelphia's

The 18-story home of the *Philadelphia Inquirer* was built in 1924. The stunning white structure topped with a gold dome and a four-faced clock tower housed not only the newspapers' offices and main newsroom but also the most modern printing plant in the world. The *Philadelphia Daily News* moved into the building in the 1950s. Both publications moved to smaller offices in 2011.

Packard Motor Car Showroom and Factory was built to impress potential customers. (Photos by Tricia Pompilio.)

Packard building. It opened in 1910. Cars were made and assembled on the building's upper floors then displayed on the glass-enclosed, two-story ground floor. The building's 1979 National Register of Historic Places application notes that: "The main auto showroom was designed to be an overwhelming and stately room appropriate to the act of purchasing a Packard Motor car ..."

"Two story high piers carry immense beams sheathed in decorative plaster, embossed with a grape vine pattern. Panels, framed with molded plaster, add to the richness of the room. The overall effect is heightened by electric chandeliers hanging from the beams."

In the 1930s, the *Philadelphia Record* took over the Packard building, and many people still refer to the structure as "the Press building." The location allowed the smaller newspaper to almost literally face-off against the *Philadelphia Inquirer*, which had its newsroom and printing presses one block north at 400 North Broad Street.

The building was renovated in the 1980s and transformed into luxury apartments.

THIS USED TO BE: Packard Motor Car Showroom and Factory

NOW IT'S: The Packard — Apartments

LOCATION: Lower North Philadelphia

Reclaiming the Riverfront

Philadelphia is the city it is today thanks to the Delaware River. The indigenous Lenni Lenape were the first to live here, settling in the area thousands of years before the arrival of the first European settlers from the Netherlands, Sweden, and Germany. The area was named "Philadelphia," from the Greek words *philos* (beloved or dear) and *adelphos* (brother or brotherly) in the 1660s by British Quaker leader William Penn, who envisioned the city as a place where all religions could worship freely.

By 1750, Philadelphia was the busiest port in North America, a commercial center where crude oil, cocoa, sugar, textiles, grain, steel, and other products fueled the growing colonies. The banks of the Delaware were dotted with manufacturing companies, refineries, warehouses, and piers. Before Ellis Island, immigrants landed at the Washington Ave. Immigration Station.

Municipal Pier 11 was built in 1896 with a two-level waterfront building that served shipping needs on its first floor with recreation space above. It was an active hub in the years when Philadelphia was known as "the Workshop of the World."

In the late 1960s, the city began reclaiming its unused docks, seeking to transform them into useable space. The nonprofit Delaware River Waterfront Corporation, the agency now charged with developing the land along the river, reopened Municipal Pier 11 to the public in 2011.

Examples of the DRWC's good work dot the Delaware River. Walk south to visit Spruce Street Harbor Park, 301 South Christopher Columbus Boulevard, and Washington Green, South Christopher Columbus Boulevard and Washington Avenue.

Race Street Pier sits in the shadow of the Benjamin Franklin Bridge. New Jersey is on the other side of the Delaware River. (Photo by Tricia Pompilio.)

The one-acre park in the shadow of the Delaware River was renamed Race Street Pier to emphasize the connection between the city and the river. The pier is now a community space where locals and visitors alike hang out, enjoy yoga classes, or spread out picnics.

THIS USED TO BE: Municipal Pier 11

NOW IT'S: Race Street Pier

LOCATION: Old City

SOURCES

Websites:
African American Museum of Philadelphia – aampmuseum.org
Alamy Stock Photos – alamy.com
All That Philly Jazz – phillyjazz.us
American Canal Society – americancanalsociety.org
American Library Association – ala.org
Association for Public Art – www.associationforpublicart.org/
The *Atlantic* magazine – www.theatlantic.com
Atlas Obscura – atlasobscura.com

The Bellevue – Philadelphia – bellevuePhiladelphia.com
Billy Penn – Billypenn.com
Blackbottom – theblackbottom.wordpress.com

Catholic Historical Research Center of Archdiocese of Philadelphia – chrc-phila.org
Cinema Treasures – cinematreasures.org
City of Philadelphia Archives – www.phila.gov
Consortium for History, Science, Technology and Medicine – www.chstm.org
Constitutional Walking Tour of Philadelphia – www.theconstitutional.com
The Cultural Landscape Foundation – tcif.org/landscapes
Curbed Philadelphia – philly.curbed.com

The Delaware River Blog – delawareriver.net

Eater Philly – philly.eater.com
Encyclopedia Britannica – www.britannica.com
Encyclopedia of Greater Philadelphia – philadelphiaencyclopedia.org
The Enterprise Center – www.theenterprisecenter.org

ExplorePAHistory – explorepahistory.com
First Presbyterian Church in Philadelphia – www.fpcphila.org
Free Library of Philadelphia – www.freelibrary.org/
Friends of Wissahickon – fow.org

Greater Philadelphia Cultural Alliance – philaculture.org
Greater Philadelphia GeoHistory Network – philageohistory.org

Hidden City Philadelphia – hiddencityphila.org
Historic Philadelphia – www.historicphiladelphia.org
The Historical Marker Database – hmdb.org
Historical Society of Philadelphia – hsp.org
The History Channel – history.com
A History of Philadelphia – localhistories.org
History of Philadelphia Watersheds and Sewers – www.phillyh2o.org
History of the Port of Philadelphia – www.philaport.com

HistoryNet – historynet.com

Kenneth W. Milano – kennethwmilano.com

Lasalle University – lasalle.edu
The Library Company of Philadelphia – librarycompany.org
Library of Congress – www.loc.gov
Loews Philadelphia – www.loewshotels.com

Mural Arts Philadelphia – www.muralarts.org

Naked Philly – www.ocfrealty.com/naked-philly-search
National Archives – archives.gov
National Constitution Center – constitutioncenter.org
National Geographic – nationalgeographic.org
National Register of Historic Places – www.nps.gov
New World Encyclopedia – www.newworldencyclopedia.org

Old Images of Philadelphia – www.facebook.com/oldimagesofphiladelphia

PA Historical Markers Program – www.phmc.pa.gov
Pennsylvania Heritage – paheritage.com
Philadelphia – www.historians.org
Philadelphia – www.phillymag.com
Philadelphia Architects and Buildings – philadelphiabuildings.org
Philadelphia Business News – bizjournals.com/philadelphia
Philadelphia Chinatown Development Corporation – chinatown-pcdc.org
Philadelphia Church Project – phillychurchproject.org
The Philadelphia Contributionship – 1972.com
Philadelphia Convention & Visitors Bureau – discoverphl.com
Philadelphia Futures – philadelphiafutures.org
Philadelphia Gayborhood Blog – thegayborhood.guru.wordpress.com
Philadelphia for History Buffs – www.wheretraveler.com
Philadelphia Historical Sites – drexel.edu
Philadelphia History – historylive.net
Philadelphia History – www.ushistory.us
Philadelphia History Collaborative – www.philaculture.com
Philadelphia History Museum at the Atwater Kent – philadelphiahistory.org
Philadelphia Museum of Art – philamuseum.org
Philadelphia Music Alliance – www.philadelphiamusicalliance.org
Philadelphia Neighborhoods – philadelphianeighborhoods.com
Philadelphia Place – philaplace.org
Philadelphia Public Art – philart.net
PhillyBite Magazine – phillybite.com
PhillyVoice – phillyvoice.com
PlanPhilly – planphilly.com
Public Broadcasting Service – pbs.org

Southwark Historical Society – southwarkhistory.org

St. Joseph's University – sju.edu
Teaching American History – teachingamericanhistory.com
Temple University – temple.edu
Theatre of the Living Arts – venue.tlaphilly.com

US National Park Service – nps.gov
University City Historic Society – www.uchs.net

Visit Philadelphia – visitphilly.com

WAMU – wamu.org
WHYY – whyy.org
WXPN – wxpn.org
Workshop of the World Philadelphia – workshopoftheworld.com
West Philadelphia Community History Center – westphillyhistory.archives.upenn.edu

Print media sources, most obtained via newspapers.com
Associated Press
The New York Times
Philadelphia Daily News
The Philadelphia Inquirer
Philadelphia Magazine
The Philadelphia Tribune
United Press International
The Washington Post

Print sources

Avery, Ron, *A Concise History of Philadelphia*. Philadelphia: Otis Books, 1999.

Boris, Alan, *Philadelphia Radio*. Charleston, SC: Arcadia Publishing, 2011.

DePilla, Michael, *South Philadelphia's Little Italy and 9th Street Italian Market*. Charleston, SC, Arcadia Publishing, 2016.

Double, Bill, *Philadelphia's Washington Square*, Charleston, SC, Arcadia Publishing, 2009.

Dubin, Murray, *South Philadelphia: Mummers, Memories, and the Melrose Diner*. Philadelphia, Temple University Press, 1996.

Elliott, Joseph E.B. Nathaniel Popkin and Peter Woodall. *Philadelphia: Finding the Hidden City*. Philadelphia, Temple University Press, 2017.

Gadomski, Michael P. Philadelphia: A Keepsake. Atglen, PA, 2019.

Golden, Jane, Robin Rice and Monica Yant Kinney, *Philadelphia Murals & Stories They Tell*. Philadelphia, Temple University Press, 2002.

Golden, Jane, Robin Rice and Natalie Pompilio, *More Philadelphia Murals and the Stories They Tell*. Philadelphia, Temple University Press, 2006.

Gross, Linda P. and Theresa R. Snyder, *Philadelphia's 1876 Centennial Exhibition*. Charleston, SC, Arcadia Publishing, 2005.

Homan, Lynn M. and Thomas Reilly, *Visiting Turn-of-the-Century Philadelphia*, Charleston, SC, Arcadia Publishing, 1999.

Keels, Thomas H., *Philadelphia's Graveyards and Cemeteries*, Charleston, SC: Arcadia Publishing, 2003.

Kyriakodis, Harry. *Philadelphia's Lost Waterfront*. Charleston, SC: Arcadia Publishing, 2011.

Kyriakodis, Harry and Joel Spivak. *Underground Philadelphia*. Charleston, SC: Arcadia Publishing, 2019.

Milano, Kenneth W. *Remembering Kensington & Fishtown*. Philadelphia's Riverward Neighborhoods. Charleston, SC: Arcadia Publishing, 2008.

Minardi, Joseph, *City of Neighborhood: Philadelphia*, 1890 – 1910. Charleston, SC: Arcadia Publishing, 2020.

Moss, Roger W. and Tom Crane. *Historic Landmarks of Philadelphia*. Philadelphia: University of Pennsylvania Press, 2008.

Nickels, Thom, *Philadelphia Architecture*. Charleston, S.C.: Arcadia Press, 2005.

Nickels, Thom. *Legendary Locals of Center City Philadelphia*. Charleston, S.C.: Arcadia Press, 2014.

Oberholtzer, Ellis Paxson Philadelphia – A History of the City and its People. Germany: Jazzybee Verlad, 2017.

Pompilio, Natalie and Tricia Pompilio. *Walking Philadelphia: 30 Walking Tours Exploring Art, Architecture, History and Little-Known Gems*. Birmingham, AL: Wilderness Press, 2017

The Print and Photograph Department of the Library Company of Philadelphia, *Center City Philadelphia in the 19th Century*. Charleston, SC: Arcadia Publishing, 2006.

Skaler, Thomas Morris. *Philadelphia's Broad Street South and North*. Charleston, SC: Arcadia Publishing, 2003.

Skaler, Thomas Morris and Thomas H. Keels, *Society Hill and Old City*. Charleston, SC: Arcadia Publishing, 2002.

Spector, Gus. *Philadelphia Neighborhoods*. Charleston, SC: Arcadia Publishing, 2008.

Williams, Peter John. *Philadelphia: The World War I Years*. Charleston, SC: Arcadia Publishing, 2013.

To determine neighborhoods, I used the *Philadelphia Inquirer*'s web mapping application built by the Delaware Valley Regional Planning Commission for https://www.dvrpc.org/webmaps/pin/index.htm

INDEX